Doggin'
The Finger Lakes

The 50 Best Places
To Hike With Your Dog

DOUG GELBERT

illustrations by

ANDREW CHESWORTH

Cruden Bay Books

There is always a new trail to look forward to...

DOGGIN' THE FINGER LAKES: THE 50 BEST PLACES
TO HIKE WITH YOUR DOG

Copyright 2007 by Cruden Bay Books

All rights reserved. No part of this book may be reproduced or
transmitted in any form or by any means, electronic or mechanical,
including photocopying, recording or by any information storage and
retrieval system without permission in writing from the Publisher.

Cruden Bay Books
PO Box 467
Montchanin, DE 19710
www.hikewithyourdog.com

International Standard Book Number 978-0-9797074-2-1

"Dogs are our link to paradise...to sit with a dog on a hillside
on a glorious afternoon is to be back in Eden,
where doing nothing was not boring - it was peace."
- Milan Kundera

Ahead On The Trail

Introduction

The Finger Lakes can be a great place to hike with your dog. Within a short drive you can be scaling mountains that leave your dog panting, exploring impossibly scenic gorges that will set tails to wagging or trotting along glacial lakes for hours.

I have selected what I consider to be the 50 best places to take your dog for an outing in the Finger Lakes and ranked them according to subjective criteria including the variety of hikes available, opportunities for canine swimming and pleasure of the walks. The rankings include a mix of parks that feature long walks and parks that contain short walks. Did I miss your favorite? Let us know at *www.hikewithyourdog. com*.

I have defined the Finger Lakes roughly to be a saddle-shaped area bordered to the north by the New York State thruway, to the west by I-390/I-86 and to the east by Route 13/I-81.

For dog owners it is important to realize that not all parks are open to our best trail companions (see page 14 for a list of parks that do not allow dogs). It is sometimes hard to believe but not everyone loves dogs. We are, in fact, in the minority when compared with our non-dog owning neighbors.

So when visiting a park always keep your dog under control and clean up any messes and we can all expect our great parks to remain open to our dogs. And maybe some others will see the light as well. *Remember, every time you go out with your dog you are an ambassador for all dog owners.*

Grab that leash and hit the trail!
DBG

Hiking With Your Dog

So you want to start hiking with your dog. Hiking with your dog can be a fascinating way to explore the Finger Lakes from a canine perspective. Some things to consider:

🐾 Dog's Health

Hiking can be a wonderful preventative for any number of physical and behavioral disorders. One in every three dogs is overweight and running up trails and leaping through streams is great exercise to help keep pounds off. Hiking can also relieve boredom in a dog's routine and calm dogs prone to destructive habits. And hiking with your dog strengthens the overall owner/dog bond.

🐾 Breed of Dog

All dogs enjoy the new scents and sights of a trail. But some dogs are better suited to hiking than others. If you don't as yet have a hiking companion, select a breed that matches your interests. Do you look forward to an entire afternoon's hiking? You'll need a dog bred to keep up with such a pace, such as a retriever or a spaniel. Is a half-hour enough walking for you? It may not be for an energetic dog like a border collie. If you already have a hiking friend, tailor your plans to his abilities.

🐾 Conditioning

Just like humans, dogs need to be acclimated to the task at hand. An inactive dog cannot be expected to bounce from the easy chair in the den to complete a 3-hour hike. You must also be physically able to restrain your dog if confronted with distractions on the trail (like a scampering squirrel or a pack of joggers). Have your dog checked by a veterinarian before significantly increasing his activity level.

🐾 Weather

Hot humid summers do not do dogs any favors. With no sweat glands and only panting available to disperse body heat, dogs are much more susceptible to heat stroke than we are. Unusually rapid panting and/or a bright red tongue are signs of heat exhaustion in your pet.

Always carry enough water for your hike. Even days that don't seem too warm can cause discomfort in dark-coated dogs if the sun is shining brightly. In cold weather, short-coated breeds may require additional attention.

🐾 Trail Hazards

Dogs won't get poison ivy but they can transfer it to you. Stinging nettle is a nuisance plant that lurks on the side of many trails and the slightest brush will deliver troublesome needles into a dog's coat. Some trails are littered with small pieces of broken glass that can slice a dog's paws. Nasty thorns can also blanket trails that we in shoes may never notice.

🐾 Ticks

You won't be able to spend much time on the trail without encountering ticks. All are nasty but the deer tick - no bigger than a pin head - carries with it the spectre of Lyme disease. Lyme disease attacks a dog's joints and makes walking painful. The tick needs to be embedded in the skin to transmit Lyme disease. It takes 4-6 hours for a tick to become embedded and another 24-48 hours to transmit Lyme disease bacteria.

When hiking, walk in the middle of trails away from tall grass and bushes. And when the summer sun fades away don't stop thinking about ticks - they remain active any time the temperature is above 30 degrees. By checking your dog - and yourself - thoroughly after each walk you can help avoid Lyme disease. Ticks tend to congregate on your dog's ears, between the toes and around the neck and head.

🐾 Water

Surface water, including fast-flowing streams, is likely to be infested with a microscopic protozoa called *Giardia*, waiting to wreak havoc on a dog's intestinal system. The most common symptom is crippling diarrhea. Algae, pollutants and contaminants can all be in streams, ponds and puddles. If possible, carry fresh water for your dog on the trail - your dog can even learn to drink happily from a squirt bottle.

⟡ Rattlesnakes and Copperheads, etc.

Rattlesnakes are not particularly aggressive animals but you should treat any venomous snake with respect and keep your distance. A rattler's colors may vary but they are recognized by the namesake rattle on the tail and a diamond-shaped head. Unless cornered or teased by humans or dogs, a rattlesnake will crawl away and avoid striking. Avoid placing your hand in unexamined rocky areas and crevasses and try and keep your dog from doing so as well. If you hear a nearby rattle, stop immediately and hold your dog back. Identify where the snake is and slowly back away.

If you or your dog is bitten, do not panic but get to a hospital or veterinarian with as little physical movement as possible. Wrap between the bite and the heart. Rattlesnakes might give "dry bites" where no poison is injected, but you should always check with a doctor after a bite even if you feel fine.

❧   Black Bears

Are you likely to see a bear while out hiking with your dog? No, it's not likely. It is, however, quite a thrill if you are fortunate enough to spot a black bear on the trail - from a distance.

Black bear attacks are incredibly rare. In the year 2000 a hiker was killed by a black bear in Great Smoky National Park and it was the first deadly bear attack in the 66-year history of America's most popular national park. It was the first EVER in the southeastern United States. In all of North America only 43 black bear mauling deaths have ever been recorded (through 1999).

Most problems with black bears occur near a campground (like the above incident) where bears have learned to forage for unprotected food. On the trail bears will typically see you and leave the area before you ever see her. What should you do if you encounter a black bear? Experts agree on three important things:

1) Never run. A bear will outrun you, outclimb you, outswim you. Don't look like prey.
2) Never get between a female bear and a cub who may be nearby feeding.
3) Leave a bear an obvious escape route.

If the bear is at least 15 feet away and notices you make sure you keep your dog close and calm. If a bear stands on its hind legs or comes closer it may just be trying to get a better view or smell to evaluate the situation. Wave your arms and make noise to scare the bear away. Most bears will quickly leave the area.

If you encounter a black bear at close range, stand upright and make yourself appear as large a foe as possible. Avoid direct eye contact and speak in a calm, assertive and assuring voice as you back up slowly and out of danger.

❧   Porcupines

Porcupines are easy for a curious dog to catch and that makes them among the most dangerous animals you may meet because an embedded quill is not only painful but can cause infection if not properly removed.

Outfitting Your Dog For A Hike

These are the basics for taking your dog on a hike:

- **Collar.**
  It should not be so loose as to come off but you should be able to slide your flat hand under the collar.

- **Identification Tags.**
  Get one with your veterinarian's phone number as well.

- **Bandanna.**
  Can help distinguish him from game in hunting season.

- **Leash.**
  Leather lasts forever but if there's water in your dog"s future, consider quick-drying nylon.

- **Water.**
  Carry 8 ounces for every hour of hiking.

I want my dog to help carry water, snacks and other supplies on the trail. Where do I start?

To select an appropriate dog pack measure your dog's girth around the rib cage. A dog pack should fit securely without hindering the dog's ability to walk normally.

Will my dog wear a pack?

Wearing a dog pack is no more obtrusive than wearing a collar, although some dogs will take to a pack easier than others. Introduce the pack by draping a towel over your dog's back in the house and then having your dog wear an empty pack on short walks. Progressively add some crumpled newspaper and then bits of clothing. Fill the pack with treats and reward your dog from the stash. Soon your dog will associate the dog pack with an outdoor adventure and will eagerly look forward to wearing it.

How much weight can I put into a dog pack?

Many dog packs are sold by weight recommendations. A healthy, well-conditioned dog can comfortably carry 25% to 33% of its body weight. Breeds prone to back problems or hip dysplasia should not wear dog packs. Consult your veterinarian before stuffing the pouches with gear.

How does a dog wear a pack?

The pack, typically with cargo pouches on either side, should ride as close to the shoulders as possible without limiting movement. The straps that hold the dog pack in place should be situated where they will not cause chafing.

What are good things to put in a dog pack?

Low density items such as food and poop bags are good choices. Ice cold bottles of water can cool your dog down on hot days. Don't put anything in a dog pack that can break. Dogs will bang the pack on rocks and trees as they wiggle through tight spots in the trail. Dogs also like to lie down in creeks and other wet spots so seal items in plastic bags. A good use for dog packs when on day hikes around the Finger Lakes is trail maintenance - your dog can pack out trash left by inconsiderate visitors before you.

🐾 *Are dog booties a good idea?*

Dog booties can be an asset, especially for the occasional canine hiker whose paw pads have not become toughened. In some places, there may be broken glass. Hiking boots for dogs are designed to prevent pads from cracking while trotting across rough surfaces. Used in winter, dog booties provide warmth and keep ice balls from forming between toe pads when hiking through snow.

🐾 *What should a doggie first aid kit include?*

Even when taking short hikes it is a good idea to have some basics available for emergencies:

- 4" square gauze pads
- cling type bandaging tapes
- topical wound disinfectant cream
- tweezers
- insect repellent - no reason to leave your dog unprotected against mosquitoes and black flies
- veterinarian's phone number

"I can't think of anything that brings me closer to tears than when my old dog - completely exhausted after a hard day in the field - limps away from her nice spot in front of the fire and comes over to where I'm sitting and puts her head in my lap, a paw over my knee, and closes her eyes, and goes back to sleep. I don't know what I've done to deserve that kind of friend."
-Gene Hill

Low Impact Hiking With Your Dog

Every time you hike with your dog on the trail you are an ambassador for all dog owners. Some people you meet won't believe in your right to take a dog on the trail. Be friendly to all and make the best impression you can by practicing low impact hiking with your dog:

- Pack out everything you pack in.

- Do not leave dog scat on the trail; if you haven't brought plastic bags for poop removal bury it away from the trail and topical water sources.

- Hike only where dogs are allowed.

- Stay on the trail.

- Do not allow your dog to chase wildlife.

- Step off the trail and wait with your dog while horses and other hikers pass.

- Do not allow your dog to bark - people are enjoying the trail for serenity.

- *Have as much fun on your hike as your dog does.*

The Other End Of The Leash

Leash laws are like speed limits - everyone seems to have a private interpretation of their validity. Some dog owners never go outside with an unleashed dog; others treat the laws as suggestions or disregard them completely. It is not the purpose of this book to tell dog owners where to go to evade the leash laws or reveal the parks where rangers will look the other way at an unleashed dog. Nor is it the business of this book to preach vigilant adherence to the leash laws. Nothing written in a book is going to change people's behavior with regard to leash laws. So this will be the last time leash laws are mentioned, save occasionally when we point out the parks where dogs are welcomed off leash.

How To Pet A Dog
Tickling tummies slowly and gently works wonders.
Never use a rubbing motion; this makes dogs bad-tempered.
A gentle tickle with the tips of the fingers is all that is necessary
to induce calm in a dog. I hate strangers who go up to dogs with their
hands held to the dog's nose, usually palm towards themselves.
How does the dog know that the hand doesn't hold something horrid?
The palm should always be shown to the dog and go straight
down to between the dog's front legs and tickle gently with
a soothing voice to accompany the action.
Very often the dog raises its back leg in a scratching movement,
it gets so much pleasure from this.
-Barbara Woodhouse

No Dogs

Before we get started on the best places to take your dog, let's get out of the way some of the trails that do not allow dogs:

Baltimore Woods - *Marcellus*
Beaver Lake Nature Center - *Baldwinsville*
Bristol Hills Trail - *Bristol*
Cayuga Nature Center - *Ithaca*
Cumming Nature Center - *Naples*
Lime Hollow Center for Environment - *Cortland*
Onanda Park - *Canandaigua*
Sandy Bottom Nature Trail - *Richmond*
Sapsucker Woods Sanctuary - *Ithaca*

O.K. That wasn't too bad. Let's forget about these and move on to some of the great places where we CAN take our dogs across the Finger Lakes...

The 50 Best Places To Hike With Your Dog In The Finger Lakes...

1
Letchworth State Park

The Park

William Pryor Letchworth entered business at the age of 15 in Auburn in 1848, working as a clerk in the saddlery and hardware trade. He soon shifted to the iron products business and was successful enough to retire at the age of 48. But he did not stop working. He became an advocate for epilectic and poor children from his post on the New York State Board of Charities, agitating tirelessly for their treatment, often with his own money.

He first bought land on the Genesee River in 1859 when he started to build his Glen Iris Estate with the help of famous landscape artist William Webster. When development of the Genesee River loomed in 1906, Letchworth scrapped plans for Glen Iris to be converted into an orphanage after his death and gave it to the State of New York instead to preserve the lands forever. A year later, and three years before William Letchworth's death, his 1,000 acres became one of the cornerstones of the New York state park system.

Livingston

Phone Number
- (585) 493-3600

Website
- nysparks.state.ny.us/parks/info.asp?parkID=12

Admission Fee
- Vehicle entrance fee May to November

Park Hours
- 6:00 a.m. to 11:00 p.m.

Nearest Finger Lake
- southwest of Conesus

Directions
- *Castile*; From I-390 take Exit 7 to the park off Route 36.

The Walks

The "Grand Canyon of the East" covers more than 14,000 acres and serves up about 70 miles of trails, many of the multi-use variety. Most folks, however, don't explore much beyond the three major waterfalls at the park hub so you will have no trouble slipping away into the woods with your dog in relative solitude. If you can, bring your dog to the *Gorge Trail* early in the morning before the crowds arrive to gape at the hydrospectaculars and admire the stone bridges and stairways created by the Civilian Conservation Corps

Bonus

In 1743 Mary Jemison was born aboard ship, bound for the New World. Her family settled near modern-day Gettysburg on the American frontier. In 1758, in the early days of the French and Indian War, the Jemison farm was raided by French and Shawnee warriors. The raiders headed west and soon killed everyone in her family except Mary. In Fort Duquesne (Pittsburgh) she was sold to Seneca Indians and renamed Dehgewanus. She lived among the Senecas, married and was led back to her husband's homeland on the Genessee River, walking 700 miles with a young son on her back. She arrived but without her husband, who fell ill and died. She would live in the valley another 70 years until the "Old White Woman of the Genesee" died in 1833 on the Buffalo Creek Reservation. Two generations later her grandchildren appealed to William Letchworth to have here remains moved to her one-time land here. He obliged, and Mary Jemison came home. You can see her grave, topped by a statue dedicated in 1910, behind the Glen Iris Inn.

during the Depression.

Good places to sneak away with your dog are behind the museum, highlighted by the *Mary Jemison Trail*, and in the northern area of the park near the campground off Schenck Road with its gorge overlooks.

Trail Sense: Well-mapped and blazed.

There is plenty for your dog to see at Letchworth State Park.

Dog Friendliness

Dogs are welcome to hike and camp but are not allowed in any park building, cabin area or swimming pool area.

Traffic

All kinds but you can seek out a quiet canine hike.

Canine Swimming

There are some side streams in the park for refreshing splashing.

Trail Time

Full days possible.

2
Lindsay–Parsons Biodiversity Preserve

The Park

As Director of the Cornell Institute for Research in Chemical Ecology Thomas Eisner was well familiar with trips to exotic locales around the world in search of beneficial plants. Born in Uruguay, he had extensive field experience on four continents.

But what about in his own backyard? Was it possible that temperate climates like that experienced in Ithaca could harbor plants with medicinal value like those hunted for in humid tropical jungles?

Dr. Eisner approached the Finger Lakes Land Trust to see if they could find an ecologically diverse tract to pursue research for useful botanical chemicals. Through significant private donations the trust was able to piece together this remarkable preserve that became the world's first temperate-zone preserve for research in chemical ecology and bio-prospecting.

Tompkins County

Phone Number
- None

Website
- www.fllt.org/protected_lands/protected_lands1.php?id=22

Admission Fee
- None

Park Hours
- Sunrise to sunset

Nearest Finger Lake
- south of Cayuga

Directions
- *West Danby*; south of town on Route 34/96. The preserve lot is on the east side of the road.

The Walks

One of the joys of hiking with your dog is watching her react to her surroundings and there is plenty to stimulate the canine senses here. Ravines, heavy brush, open meadows, beaver ponds, stands of hemlock and pine, marshes, glacially carved hillside, oak-hickory forests are all on the hiking menu at Lindsay-Parsons Biodiversity Preserve.

The star walk here is the *Blue Trail* that mixes open meadows with long views of the surrounding hills and a hillside woodland loop. The full tour of

Bonus
Celia's Cup, named for the wife of a preserve benefactor, is a large depression hollowed by a mighty chunk of glacial ice. It makes ian easy-to-see example of the region's "kettle and kame" topography. Kettles can contain a number of different ecosystems. Celia's Cup is a dry, unforested kettle.

the *Blue Trail* will take about an hour but you will want to mix in trips along *Red Trail* and *Yellow Trail* to get the full effect of the preserve. This is a sporty track, down one side of a wide valley and up the other. The property is drained by the Cayuga Outlet creating plenty of soft, paw-friendly soil under paw.

Trail Sense: There is a helpful educational kiosk and a map to take with you. The trails are well-blazed and imaginative.

Dog Friendliness
Dogs are welcome on these trails.

Traffic
More than you typically expect at a Finger Lakes Land Trust preserve but usually far from crowded; foot traffic only.

Canine Swimming
Coleman Lake is the most obvious spot for a refresher.

Trail Time
More than one hour.

3
Fillmore Glen State Park

The Park

Dr. Charles Atwood, a local physician by vocation and a botanist by avocation, is the "Father of Fillmore Glen." A member of the Finger Lakes State Parks Commission since it was formed in 1924, he led the preservationist movement to create this park.

The area was well-known and appreciated by the locals for its wide range of botanical wonders. Trails were open in the glen for years before it became a jewel of the Empire State park system in 1925.

The glen is named for Millard Fillmore, 13th president of the United States, born down the road in Summerhill. The park today covers 941 acres.

Cayuga County

Phone Number
- (315) 497-0130

Website
- nysparks.state.ny.us/parks/info.asp?parkID=35

Admission Fee
- Vehicle entrance fee May to November

Park Hours
- Daylight hours

Nearest Finger Lake
- southeast of Owasco

Directions
- *Moravia*; one mile south of the village on Route 38.

The Walks

The main canine hiking experience at Fillmore Glen is on the *Gorge Trail* that crosses Dry Creek on nine bridges and visits five major waterfalls. Much of the elaborate stonework along the trail was constructed by Civilian Conservation Corps stonemasons during the Great Depression. This is an easy trot for your dog for two miles into the glen, starting flat and becoming increasingly steep as you reach the end of the gorge. Note that the *Gorge Trail* is closed in the winter and stays very wet after a recent rain.

To complete a hiking loop back to the parking area you have two choices - the *South Rim Trail* and the *North Rim Trail*. The south rim route is the more benign of the two as it connects several picnic pavilions. The heartier canine hike is through the hemlocks on the higher side of the gorge, the north side. The most scenic side waterfall drops from this side.

Bonus

Millard Fillmore was the first president born when George Washington was no longer alive and the last president who was neither a Democrat nor a Republican (he was a Whig). Fillmore was also the first non-elected President, ascending to office from the vice-presidency in July 1850 with the death of Zachary Taylor. Interestingly, he then served as President without a Vice-President. Fillmore supported the Compromise of 1850 that admitted California as a free state but also established a stricter slave law that was so controversial he was not even nominated by his own party to run for President again in 1852. Millard Fillmore was born in a log cabin five miles from the park in 1800 and a replica of the cabin constructed from similar materials is on display by the parking lot.

Trail Sense: A park map is available and the gorge and trails are marked by signage.

Dog Friendliness

Dogs are allowed throughout the park, including the campground, save for the bathing areas.

Traffic

Foot traffic only in the gorge.

Canine Swimming

Your dog will enjoy the natural swimming pool beyond the Cowsheds, a magazine cover-worthy waterfall that drops into a semi-circular ampitheatre.

A replica cabin of the one Millard Fillmore grew up in is located in his namesake park.

Trail Time

Several hours of trail time are available.

4
Wesley Hill
Nature Preserve

The Park

Briggs Gully is one of the Finger Lakes' biggest gorges. Its steep sides managed to defy some loggers although penty of timber was felled here to feed the hungry Frosttown sawmills nearby.

In 1926 three young Rochester artists - John C. Wenrich, James Havens and Colburn Dugan - bought a 90-acre slice of Briggs Gully as a place to come for relaxation and inspiration. In 1999 the Finger Lakes Trust was able to make this retreat the core of the Wesley Hill Nature Preserve. Additional purchases have increased the preserve's size to around 400 acres.

Ontario County

Phone Number
- None

Website
- www.fllt.org/protected_lands/protected_lands1.php?id=31

Admission Fee
- None

Park Hours
- Sunrise to sunset

**Nearest Finger Lake
- east of Honeoye**

Directions
- *Honeoye*; from town, head east on Route 20A and go south on East Lake Road. Take a left on Pine Hill Road and then a right, following signs for Cummings Nature Center. The road becomes Gulick Road and you are close to two preserve parking areas. Make a right on Wesley Road to one area or stay on Gulick about one mile past Wesley to the other.

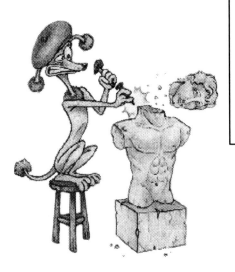

22

Bonus

The most accomplished of the triumverate of original artist-owners was James Dexter Havens.

The son of a United States Congressman and head of the legal department for Eastman Kodak in Rochester, Havens was stricken by juvenile diabetes at the age of 14 in 1914. Doctors gave him only two years to live but he clung to life, bedridden, for eight years.

At that point, through his father's contacts, young Jim Havens became the first American to undergo insulin therapy. By the time he received treatment, he weighed less than 74 pounds at the age of twenty-two. The treatment worked and Havens went on to live a relatively normal life until he died in 1960.

Having taken up drawing to relieve boredom during his illness, Havens first made his mark in the art world as a printmaker and was elected an Associate of the National Academy in 1951.

The Walks

This a paradise for an active dog to hike. A quintet of well-blazed, interesting trails cover over six miles and visit all corners of the preserve. The star hike here, accessed from the Gulick Road lot, is the red-blazed *Rim Trail* that bounds through mature forests, visits a woodland pond, plunges into old growth stands of white pine and white oak, explores some side gullies, traces the rim of Briggs Gully and arrives at the Wenrich Cabin before looping back to the parking area for a trip of almost three miles.

To explore different habitats you can start at Wesley Road where more recently abandoned farms are in various stages of reforesting. Oh, yes. There are are arresting views of the Honeoye to be had from rock outcrops on the north rim of Briggs Gully. There is plenty of room for your dog to stretch out on these generous, dirt trails.

Trail Sense: Map/brochures are available at the trailhead and the trails are blazed. Stay alert for trail switches at intersections.

Dog Friendliness
Dogs are allowed to hike these trails.
Traffic
No horse and no bikes.
Canine Swimming
There is easy access to the woodland pond from grassy banks.
Trail Time
About a half-day.

5
Cornell
Plantations

The Park

The stated purpose of the Cornell Plantations is "to hold, manage, protect, and enhance the living botanical collections and the natural areas and gorges of Cornell for the benefit and use of the university community and the public."

Cornell Plantations officially came into existence in 1944, when Liberty Hyde Bailey coined the name. Most of the gardens and the arboretum have been developed since the early 1970s. Cornell maintains nearly 3,000 acres in formal gardens and natural areas.

The Walks

A college campus is often a great place to seek a canine hike with your dog, especially when class is not in session. When the campus grounds are as spectacular as Cornell University's, it is simply a bonus.

The Cornell Plantations are a beguiling mix of landscaped grounds and natural areas. The backbone of the Plantations are 14 specialty gardens dispersed around Plantations Road. Dogs are not often permitted in public flower gardens so it is a rare treat to hike with your dog through these 25 acres of plantings. The same can be said for arboretums and your dog can enjoy the 150-acre F.R. Newman Arboretum here, trotting on serpentine paths through collections of shrubs and native New York trees.

Across Fall Creek your dog can explore such natural areas as Hemlock Grove across the stone Sackett Bridge, easily reached by foot. Pop out on the wrong trail and you may wind up on the Cornell University golf course, designed by

Tompkins County

Phone Number
- 607-255-2400

Website
- www.plantations.cornell.edu

Admission Fee
- None

Park Hours
- Sunrise to sunset

**Nearest Finger Lake
- southeast of Cayuga**

Directions
- *Ithaca*; on the Cornell campus. From Dryden Road (Route 366) turn onto Judd Falls Road. Take the jughandle exit down to Plantations Road and turn right to the Visitor Center.

Bonus

Ezra Cornell, founder of the university, created Beebe Lake in 1839 by building Triphammer Dam. He named the lake for Colonel Jeremiah S. Beebe, who hired Cornell shortly after he came to Ithaca in 1828.
The lake provided reliable water for Beebe's plaster and flour mills at the base of Ithaca Falls.
The water flowed to the mills through a tunnel Cornell blasted out of the south side of Falls Creek Gorge using black powder.

Robert Trent Jones, America's pre-eminent golf course designer at the time. If so, check out his massive trademark greens.

You can also hike with your dog around Beebe Lake with just a minimum of streetwalking. Another unusual natural area is the greenway from campus into downtown Ithaca through the Cascadilla Creek gorge. This trail, "connecting town and gown," covers 1.3 miles and many stairs.

Trail Sense: The Finger Lakes' most beautiful map/brochure will guide you around but if you are of a botanical bent a purchase of *Cornell Plantations Path Guide* from the gift shop is a must.

Dog Friendliness
Dogs are welcome in Cornell Plantations.
Traffic
Plenty of bikes, strollers and trail users everywhere but it is not difficult to find a quiet place.
Canine Swimming
There are places for your dog to reach the waters of Beebe Lake and Fall Creek.
Trail Time
A half day possible.

6
Robert H. Treman State Park

The Park

Enfield Creek has been especially busy here. A perfectly good gorge was filled in by glacial debris after the most recent Ice Age 10,000 years ago and the little stream had to get started again, carving a whole new gorge. In the lower part of the park it started by unearthing the previous gully but as it reached the upper park the creek got tired and gouged out a new path in the bedrock. So Enfield Glen today is a mix of the old and the really old.

In 1920 Robert H. Treman, an outstanding baseball pitcher at Cornell in the 1870s and later Deputy Governor of the Federal Reserve Bank of New York, donated 387 acres in Enfield Glen to the State. In 1924, the property came under the auspices of the newly formed Finger Lakes State Parks Commission with Treman at the helm.

Tompkins County

Phone Number
- (607) 273-3440

Website
- nysparks.state.ny.us/parks/ info.asp?parkID=104

Admission Fee
- Vehicle entrance fee May to November, although you can hike into the park on the *Finger Lakes Trail*

Park Hours
- Daylight hours

Nearest Finger Lake
- southwest of Cayuga

Directions
- *Ithaca*; 5 miles southwest of town on Enfield Falls Road (Route 327) off Route 13.

When he died in 1938 his favorite park was named in his memory. The nearby Allan H. Treman State Marine Park is named for his son.

The Walks

This is not the place to bring your dog for a casual hike (unless you just want to sneak down for a look at the 115-foot Lucifer Falls and return up the *Red Pine Trail*). There are only two main trails, parallel two-mile routes down the Enfield Gorge. From the Upper Park you would be best advised to take the *Rim Trail* down to the bottom of the gorge for two reasons; first, you'll be hiking upstream on the return up the *Gorge Trail* so you get longer looks at the waterfalls and

> ## Bonus
> Still standing in the Upper Park is the "Old Mill," built by 36-year old Isaac Knapp Rumsey in 1839 to grind meal. The water-powered mill spurred development of the hamlet of Enfield Falls. Complete with original machinery, the mill was restored in the 1920s.
> And an additional bonus is another set of falls you may have missed - located behind the mill where Fish Kill Creek tumbles to meet Enfield Creek.

second, your dog will go down the many steps of the amazing Cliff Staircase, not up.

But any way you explore Enfield Gorge will be a winner. The Civilian Conservation Corps did some of its most impressive stonework in the gorge to make it passable. The *Gorge Trail* mostly climbs steadily but

Your dog wll appreciate the stonework in Enfield Gorge.

the *Rim Trail* rolls up and down, actually touching the creek at times. Both these trails close in November until the ice clears in the spring; the *Finger Lakes Trail* that runs through three miles of the southern part of the park stays open through the winter.

Trail Sense: A trailmap is available and will come in handy locating the *Rim Trail* in the camping area.

Dog Friendliness
Dogs are allowed on the trails and in the campground but not in the swimming area or in the cabins.

Traffic
Foot traffic only in the gorge.

Canine Swimming
There are places for your dog to swim safely in Enfield Creek from both the *Gorge Trail and the Rim Trail.*

Trail Time
Allow three hours to complete the loop in the Enfield Glen.

7
Danby
State Forest

The Park

After hiking long distance trails in New England in 1961, Wallace D. Wood of Rochester proposed a similar trail to the Genesee Valley Hiking Club and the *Finger Lakes Trail* (FLT) across New York's scenic southern tier was born. The precise route would be left to local clubs.

The next year the Cayuga Trails Club in Ithaca won sponsorship of 70 miles of the new FLT. The club used a low-flying airplane to scout possible trail routes, flying through Michigan Hollow here at 500 feet before deciding on an appropriate trail corridor.

For several years, Cliff and Doris Abbott of the Cayuga Trails Club had a vision to create the first loop trail of the Finger Lakes Trail System. After several years of planning, negotiating, flagging route, clearing trail, building foot bridges, and marking the final route, the *Abbott Loop Trail* was officially inaugurated in Danby State Forest in 1992.

Tompkins County

Phone Number
- None

Website
- None

Admission Fee
- None

Park Hours
- Sunrise to sunset

**Nearest Finger Lake
- south of Cayuga**

Directions
- *Danby*; take Route 96B south out of Ithaca and continue south to the town of Danby, (about 6 miles). Go .5 mile past Danby Market and turn right on Michigan Hollow Road (unpaved) to *Abbott Loop*. The trail can also be accessed from Hill Road and Bald Hill Road (both seasonal).

The Walks

The *Abbott Loop* is a 6.7-mile detour off the main *Finger Lakes Trail* for a total circuit of 8.4 miles. Along the way you will cross three ravines and tag four hilltops, the most prominent being the westernmost, Thatcher's Pinnacle. It is a hearty 200-foot climb to the overlook off Bald Hill Road. On a clear day the village of West Danby and the Lindsay-Parsons Biodiversity Preserve spread before you.

28

Bonus

In the fall of 1965 the Cayuga Trails Club purchased the Tamarack Lean-to from the New York State Conservation Department and moved it piece-by-piece from Lampeer, NY to its current location on the FLT in the Danby State Forest, west of Route 96B. The cornerstone of Tamarack Lean-to was laid on October 10, 1965, in a ceremony described by a local radio station as "perhaps the first time in the history of the world that a cornerstone was laid for a lean-to." The cornerstone at the trail shelter contained a Cayuga Trails Club emblem, an FLTC emblem, the October issue of Cayuga Trails, two 1964 pennies, some trading stamps, and orange and white flags used to mark the trail.

There are plenty of up and downs on this track and some steep stretches but nothing an energetic dog can't handle. If you sense your dog flagging after a couple of hours on the trail, however, there are several dirt roads you can use to shorten your loop. On the other hand, if you are looking for a full-day canine hike, there is a connector from the Pinnacle that leads to the trail system of the Lindsay-Parsons Biodiversity Preserve.

Trail Sense: The _Abbot Loop_ is blazed in orange and signed; the _Finger Lakes Trail_ is blazed in white.

Dog Friendliness
Dogs are allowed to hike in the Danby State Forest.

Traffic
No bikes or horses allowed on the Finger Lakes Trail segments in the forest; this is a popular route but there will be stretches of an hour or more when you won't see another trail user.

Canine Swimming
Streams and beaver ponds will provide a refreshing break from the trail.

Trail Time
Allow four to five hours to complete the _Abbott Loop_.

8
Ganondagan
State Historic Site

The Park

The Seneca Nation was the largest of the Confederacy of Five Nations during the 17th century, extending from Lake Ontario down into Pennsylvania. The Senecas traded widely and prospered. Here on this hill they established a great granary and the town that grew up nearby, Gannagaro, was one of the largest in the Nation.

They were successful enough in the fur trade of the day to cause the French, under the Marquis de Denonville, Governor of New France, to send an army from Canada to destroy the Seneca competition. In 1687, 3,000 French soldiers invaded and burned the town, including the granary. The Senecas dispersed and would go on to build smaller villages but never again a town on the scale of Gannagaro, now known as Ganondagan.

Ontario County

Phone Number
- (585) 924-5848

Website
- www.ganondagan.org

Admission Fee
- None

Park Hours
- 8:00 a.m. to sunset

Nearest Finger Lake
- northwest of Canandaigua

Directions
- *Victor*; from the New York State Thruway Exit 45 take Route 96 into Victor. At Maple Avenue (Route 444) in the center of town, turn right and proceed south to Boughton Hill Road and turn right at the flashing red light to the site on the right.

The Walks

There is some super canine hiking on hand at Ganondagan but bring a patient dog with you because these trails are stuffed with interpretive signs. The *Earth Is Our Mother Trail*, for instance, is detailed with 29 signs across its two-mile course. The names of plants important to the Nation are listed with both their English and Seneca names.

The *Trail of Peace* is a beautiful mown grass path that recounts the story of Seneca life here and the invasion and destruction of the town. Aside from the gentle, paw-friendly track the highlight here are the views across the surrounding countryside. Down the road (park in the grass across from Murray Road) you

Bonus

The Seneca came to be known as Haudenosaunee -
"the people who build houses." Those houses were
communal longhouses covered with elm bark.
Pine pitch was smeared across the pieces of elm
to waterproof the house. The Senecas lashed bitternut
hickory trees together for the house frame.
The inner bark of the shagbark hickory was boiled to
soften it and then twisted into cord to tie sheets of
bark to rafters and posts. The interior was covered
with white birch bark to reflect light and brighten the
living space. A demonstration Bark Longhouse of the
Seneca was built at Ganondagan in 1998.

can explore Fort Hill, site of the palisaded granary. Your dog's four-wheel drive will come in handy here, as it will in several places in the historic site as you hike across the steep hills.

The trail system also connects to the six-mile *Seneca Trail* that leads back into Victor so you can make this a BIG outing for your dog - and

The Bark Longhouse was the trademark of a Seneca town.

he won't be in any hurry to leave this special place.

Trail Sense: There are descriptive map brochures and the trails are well-marked.

Dog Friendliness
Dogs are allowed to hike these historic trails.
Traffic
The trails are for foot traffic only and seldom crowded.
Canine Swimming
The Great Brook gurgles through the property but it is not a canine swimming mecca.
Trail Time
Several hours possible.

9
Taughannock Falls State Park

The Park

The Ithaca Council of the Boy Scouts of America was born in 1920 and three years later established its first summer camp here on an undeveloped parcel along Taughannock Creek, Camp Barton. The "father" of Camp Barton was Sam Bogan, the first Council Executive hired by the fledgling council and the camp was staffed by a number of Cornell University professors, including famed American ornithologist and illustrator Louis Agassiz Fuertes. When he was killed in an automobile accident four years later, the Ithaca Council was renamed "Louis Aggasiz Fuertes Council" at the request of the Scouts themselves.

After the 1926 season, however, the State of New York purchased the site of Camp Barton to create Taughannock Falls State Park (the name "Taughannock" comes from the Delaware Indians, roughly meaning "great fall in the woods"). That fall would be Taughannock Falls whose single drop of 215 feet is 33 feet higher than Niagara and higher than all but one cataract east of the Rocky Mountains.

Tompkins County

Phone Number
- (607) 387-6739

Website
- nysparks.state.ny.us/parks/info.asp?parkID=93

Admission Fee
- Vehicle entrance fee May to November

Park Hours
- Sunrise to sunset

Nearest Finger Lake
- west shore of Cayuga

Directions
- *Ulysses*; eight miles north of Ithaca on Route 89.

The Walks

Unlike its gorge kin in the Finger Lakes the easy canine hike here is the *Gorge Trail* that travels up to the falls on a wide, flat path. The more challenging fare is up on the rims. The grade is so gentle that the *Gorge Trail* remains open even through the winter. It is .75 miles under towering shade trees to the fine mist rising out of the plunge pool; you will need to retrace your steps to return on this extremely agreeable canine hike.

Bonus
Your dog won't find great swaths of groomed grass anywhere in the Finger Lakes like the ones beside Cayuga Lake. Perfect for a game of Frisbee or big game of fetch. Or, to just sit with your dog.

How's this place for a great game of fetch?

Adventurous canine hikers will want to head up the rim trails that form a 2.6-mile loop to the top and across the gorge. You will gain about 400 feet in elevation for which you purchase splendid views overlooking the gorge. The trails don't hug the edges but are close enough to give your dog pause in spots.

Trail Sense: A park map will direct you where you want to go.

Dog Friendliness
Dogs are allowed on all these trails.

Traffic
Foot traffic only; taking your dog up the rim trails will leave the casual sightseers behind.

Canine Swimming
There is splashing to be had in Taughannock Creek below the falls and access to Cayuga Lake, especially in the northern section of the park.

Trail Time
More than one hour.

10
Keuka Lake Outlet Trail

The Park

Jemima Wilkinson was a tall, young woman with a magnetic personality but seemed destined to be remembered only by her family in Cumberland, Rhode Island when she fell mortally ill at the age of 24 in 1776. She revived, and spurred by her near-death experience Wilkinson formed the "Universal Friends," America's first evangelical congregation led by a woman.

She arrived at Keuka Lake with 24 followers in 1790. Soon she boasted a following of 260 in about equal numbers from Pennsylvania and New England and thus the town of Penn Yan. Her sect did not long survive her death but by then settlers had discovered the industrial advantages of the 274-foot drop int he watercourse between Keuka and Seneca lakes.

Yates County

Phone Number
- None

Website
- www.keukaoutlettrail.net

Admission Fee
- None

Park Hours
- Sunrise to sunset

**Nearest Finger Lake
- northeast shore of Keuka to the west shore of Seneca**

Directions
- *Dresden and Penn Yan*; off Route 54A in Penn Yan on Cherry Street north of the bridge and Routes 14 & 54 on the south side of Seneca Street in Dresden.

The Crooked Lake Canal opened in 1833 to transport goods between the two lakes but it was destined to fail. It took 27 locks to smooth out the six-mile, six-hour trip. Imagine a canal boat taking three times as long to cover the distance as you and your dog would take!

The Walks

Your canine hike on the *Keuka Lake Outlet Trail* is on the railbed of the Penn Yan and New York Railway that opened on the former canal towpath. As you mosey along, take note of all the twists and turns you make and you will know how the line got the nickname "Corkscrew Railway." The trains ran until 1972 when Hurricane Agnes washed out the tracks.

In 1981 a group of volunteers purchased the land and built a trail that is a

Bonus

The first mill established on the Keuka Lake Outlet was Seneca Mills, built at the impressive falls where water crashed over shelves of limestone. At one time as many as 40 mills were siphoning water from the stream to power grist and flour mills, sawmills, distilleries, fulling mills, paper mills, and more. The only mill still operating on the Outlet Creek today is Birkett Mill in Penn Yan, the world's leading producer of buckwheat products. They have been grinding wheat from this location since 1797. On September 27, 1987, they cooked the world's biggest pancake - more than 28 feet across. The record stood until 1994 when a 46-footer, containing some two million calories, stole the Big Pancake crown.

notch above its rails-to-trails cousins. The embedded stone path favors bikes but will not grind at your dog's paws. Nature has reclaimed the industrial passageway with a vengeance - the route is well-shaded and scenic, punctuated by dramatic waterfalls. And there is the vestige of that serpentine roadbed of the railway - you will likely forget you are hiking down an old railroad right-of-way. The linear park stretches six miles so the 274-foot elevation drop goes down easy. If you don't have a car shuttle there are seven access points that will allow you to visit the *Keuka Lake Outlet Trail* in hikeable chunks.

The Seneca Mills Falls are truly worth a look.

Trail Sense: There are brochures with a map at various access points.

Dog Friendliness
Dogs are allowed and poop bags are provided.
Traffic
This popular trail is smooth enough for road bikes.
Canine Swimming
There is easy access to the Outlet Creek and sometimes deep enough for dog paddling.
Trail Time
More than one hour.

11

Finger Lakes National Forest

The Park

In 1790 the Federal government gave away this former Iroquois land in 600-acre lots to Revolutionary War veterans. Settlers came, cleared the land and after 100 years of grinding a living out of marginal soils, mostly left. Between 1890 and 1930 more than half the farms and over a million acres of farmland were abandoned in south central New York State.

Back came the Federal government. Between 1938 and 1941, over 100 farms were purchased in the area now in the National Forest. As this was done on a farm-by-farm basis not everyone was willing to sell, so today the forest lands are here and not there and sometimes over that way.

In 1982 the forest was shuffled among federal agencies and became the Finger Lakes National Forest, New York's only national forest and America's smallest.

Schuyler County

Phone Number
- (607) 546-4470

Website
- www.fs.fed.us/r9/gmfl/fingerlakes/index.htm

Admission Fee
- None

Park Hours
- Sunrise to sunset

**Nearest Finger Lake
- east of Seneca**

Directions
- *Hector*; forest headquarters are at 5218 State Route 414, north of Watkins Glen. To reach the *Interloken Trail*, turn right on Schuyler County Route 2, a half-mile north of the Ranger Station. Follow CR 2 for 4.0 miles until you reach the Blueberry Patch Campground and parking area.

The Walks

The main activity in Finger Lakes National Forest takes place on the orange-blazed *Interloken Trail* that runs 12 miles north-to-south up the spine of the park's largest contiguous tract of land. This is really an easy go for your dog as it weaves through second-growth forest and old-time pastureland. With a car shuttle you could complete the entire route or use the many intersecting trails to create loops of varying duration. Horses are only allowed in the southern

Bonus

The National Forest currently manages 1,400 acres as shrubland, a relatively uncommon habitat in the Finger Lakes. For canine hikers this means stretches of open-air travel with long views and maybe a bit of sunshine on the neck. Management is designed to maintain and promote fruit production so you may be able to pluck a blueberry or two in your travels.

sections where the terrain is a bit steeper; bikes and horses are both allowed north of Teeter Pond.

Canine hikers may prefer a tour on the 1.25-mile *Gorge Trail* (Mark Smith Road off Route 79) or the *Ravine Trail* (at the Blueberry Patch Campground) that are reserved for foot traffic only. These are kinder, gentler gorges than the other nearby gullies. The stream's work is less frenetic here and the soft dirt trail works along a rounded hillside. Both link with the *Interloken Trail* for an extendeded exploration of the forest.

The Gorge Trail here is more manageable for dogs than its wilder sister gorges.

Trail Sense: The trails are well-blazed and the reliable map park map will guide you to the trailheads.

Dog Friendliness
Dogs are allowed on the trails and in the campground.

Traffic
The forest is modestly visited, mostly in autumn. About half the trails are multi-use with several miles of hiker-only paths.

Canine Swimming
Ponds along the *Interloken Trail* are ideal doggie swimming holes; the streams are better suited for splashing or sitting.

Trail Time
A full day possible.

12
Hammond Hill State Forest

The Park

The Great Depression of the 1930s was bad for people, good for trees. In New York State, land that had been cleared for generations could no longer support families and people moved away and abandoned farms. The State Reforestation Law of 1929 and the Hewitt Amendment of 1931 set forth the legislation which authorized the Conservation Department to acquire land by gift or purchase for reforestation areas. These Reforestation Areas, consisting of not less than 500 acres of contiguous land, were to be forever devoted to "reforestation and the establishment and maintenance thereon of forests for watershed protection, the production of timber, and for recreation and kindred purposes".

The bottom line: New York had some 20% forest cover in 1930; today it has over 62%.

Tompkins County

Phone Number
- None

Website
- None

Admission Fee
- None

Park Hours
- Sunrise to sunset

**Nearest Finger Lake
- southeast of Cayuga**

Directions
- *Dryden*; from Route 13 about 2 miles west of town turn south on Irish Settlement Road. Take the third left onto Hammond Hill Road, bear right at the Y where Hammond Hill and Star Stanton roads converge. Park in the gravel lot on the right, just past the top of the hill.

The Hammond Hill State Forest is a typical reforested property. Between 1935 and 1940 Civilian Conservation Corps workers planted 708,000 pine, spruce, larch, sugar maple, white ash and red oak seedlings on the former crop-fields. Today 3,618 acres are heavily forested.

The Walks

There are no great destinations in Hammond Hill State Forest. No great views, no sparkling waterfalls, no deep lakes. Just a great place to get out and hike with your dog. If you can't find a suitable trail here, you aren't trying.

Bonus
Unlike most other Finger Lakes state forests at Hammond Hill there is an easy place to park, a defined trailhead, a trailmap and an a groomed trail system.

The trail system is elaborate. Sixteen designated trails can be combined in any number of combinations for however long you want to stay out with your dog. Each trail is labeled for beginner, intermediate or advanced and although the ratings are for skiers you can translate into hilly terrain from their guide.

The trails are natural using old farm roads and single track and shady most of the way around the state forest.

Trail Sense: A detailed trailmap is available at the trailhead and the trails are well-marked.

Dog Friendliness
Dogs are allowed to hike along these trails.

Traffic
Only the *Finger Lakes Trail* is for foot traffic alone, otherwise you might encounter anything out there. Hammond is an extremely popular winter trail fro skis and snowmobiles and a must-do for mountain bikes.

Canine Swimming
This is a hiking destination primarily.

Trail Time
Many hours possible.

13
Buttermilk Falls State Park

The Park

The Tutelo Indians resided from the eastern edge of the Blue Ridge Mountains of Virginia down to the valleys of the Mayo and Dan Rivers in North Carolina. In the 1740s, remnants of the Saponi, Tutelo, and Occaneechi Indians sought the protection of the Iroquois Confederacy after dust-ups with the Algonkians. Collectively known as the Tutelo, they settled among the Cayuga in 1753, building a small cluster of wooden cabins near the falls. Their village of Coreorgonel was one of many Iroquois towns destroyed during the Sullivan Expedition of 1779.

Like their neighboring namesake park, the initial funds for Buttermilk Falls State Park came from Robert and Laura Treman in 1924.

Tompkins County

Phone Number
- (607) 273-5761

Website
- nysparks.state.ny.us/parks/info.asp?parkID=25

Admission Fee
- Vehicle entrance fee May to November

Park Hours
- Sunrise to sunset

Nearest Finger Lake - south of Cayuga

Directions
- *Ithaca*; take Route 13 South to park entrance.

The Walks

It takes two separate glens for the Buttermilk Creek to storm 600 feet down the Cayuga Valley. You can circle the lower gorge that climaxes in the wide curtain waterfall at the bottom on two 3/4-mile trails on either side of the gorge. The north side is natural going through a shady hemlock forest while the south side utilizes a dramatic stone staircase.

After that rollick adventure the remainder of canine hiking at Buttermilk Falls is relatively tame, but nonetheless desirable. The upper section of the park (on West King Street if you are driving, not hiking) features views of the gorge and an easy trek at Lake Treman, surrounded by a 1.5-mile trail. The 25-acre lake was built in 1930.

Bonus
Near the top of the Gorge Trail you'll pass by a dark
spot shaded by a ragged 40-foot pillar of shale in
Buttermilk Creek known as Pinnacle Rock.
The rock has stood tall while all about it, literally,
has fallen victim to the powerful stream waters.

About 100 yards south of the main entrance, accessed off Sand Bank Road, you can take your dog on a gentle wetland loop on the *Larch Meadow Nature Trail*. This is the only trail at Buttermilk that will stay open during the winter and when ice lingers even later in the gorge.

Trail Sense: A park map will take you to the assorted trailheads. The trails are blazed once you reach them.

Dog Friendliness
Dogs are allowed to hike the trails around Buttermilk Falls.
Traffic
Most of the summer traffic here is for the swimming below the falls; the trails other than the gorge walk are not heavily used.
Canine Swimming
Below Buttemilk Falls when the swimming pool is closed and Lake Treman are excellent places for canine aquatics.
Trail Time
About an hour.

Your dog will earn a rest after hiking the gorge at Buttermilk Falls.

14
Monkey Run/
Cayuga Trail

The Park

The 500 acres of the Monkey Run Natural Area were acquired by Cornell University over a period of years from 1908 to 1926. It is managed as woodland, agricultural field and pine plantation.

The Cayuga Trails Club started building the *Cayuga Trail* in 1964; it now runs on both sides of Fall Creek through Monkey Run.

The Walks

The *Cayuga Trail* is a long loop that takes canine hikers along the high banks and water's edge of Fall Creek. There are vigorous climbs to many steep clifftops and unprotected views down to the water. Keep a close rein on an exuberant dog.

The trail is mostly paw-friendly dirt (susceptible to wet conditions) through hardwood forests, pine plantations, and blankets of lush ferns. Part of the trail utilizes the abandoned right-of-way of a railroad that once hauled coal into Cornell's power plant.

There is a pleasing mix of open air and shaded forest hiking for your dog along the *Cayuga Trail*. There are many options to crafting the duration of your time here, up to six miles.

Trail Sense: The trail is reliably blazed in orange.

Tompkins County

Phone Number
- (607) 255-2400

Website
- www.plantations.cornell.edu/collections/natareas/Public/Monkey/Monkey.htm

Admission Fee
- None

Park Hours
- Sunrise to sunset

Nearest Finger Lake
- east of Cayuga

Directions
- *Ithaca*; take Route 366 East. Turn left on Monkey Run Road. Continue beyond the abandoned railroad right-of-way to a small parking area at the bottom of the hill. The beginning of the *Cayuga Trail* is one mile north of downtown Ithaca at the Stewart Avenue bridge over Fall Creek.

Bonus

Fall Creek is spanned by several pedestrian bridges, including a pair of suspension bridges. Downstream, below Beebe Lake, the present bridge is the second on the site, replacing a narrower wooden suspension bridge in 1960. The current bridge hangs exactly 138 feet, 3 1/2 inches above the water.

Dog Friendliness

Dogs are not allowed on the College of Agriculture and Life Sciences Research Farmland tract.

Traffic

No bikes or horses allowed on this busy trail.

Canine Swimming

Not the ideal spot, but possible.

Trail Time

More than one hour.

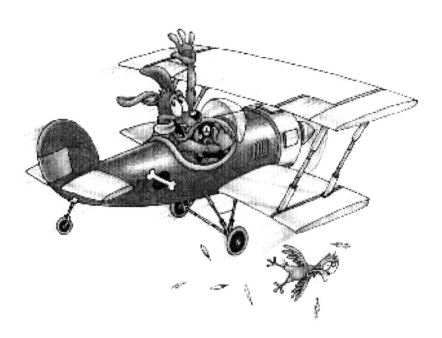

15
Ellis Hollow
Nature Preserve

The Park

John and Peleg Ellis, two brothers, left Rhode Island as young men and headed west for Herkimer County. It wasn't far enough west for Peleg, however, and he traded his Herkimer property for lot no. 84, originally assigned to Dr. Samuel Cook, a surgeon in the Revolution. At the age of 24 in 1799, Peleg came to survey his land, the area surrounding today's intersection of Ellis Hollow and Ellis Hollow Creek Roads. He cleared the woods and the next year brought his wife and two daughters to the hollow.

Peleg Ellis, who was born the year the Revolution started and died less than two years before the Civil War, was a captain of the early state militia in Dryden. He volunteered with his entire company during the War of 1812 where he became a major.

He built the family home at the headwaters of Cascadilla Creek and that house is the front half of "Head-

Tompkins County
Phone Number - None
Website - www.fllt.org/protected_ lands/protected_lands1. php?id=15
Admission Fee - None
Park Hours - Sunrise to sunset
Nearest Finger Lake - southeast of Cayuga
Directions - *Dryden*; from Ithaca follow Ellis Hollow Road 2.5 miles past East Hill Shopping Plaza. Turn left on Genung Road, then right on Ellis Hollow Creek Road. The preserve entrance is located on the left side of road, just past the creek.

waters" at 1735 Ellis Hollow Road. Barbara Keeton's family were not residents of Ellis Hollow quite that long ago but loved it just the same and donated the land for this 111-acre preserve to the Finger Lakes Land Trust to remain unspoiled and available for quiet recreation.

Bonus
The preserve is home to some particularly impressive cucumber trees, a large member of the magnolia family and the only one native to the Finger Lakes. The cucumber tree sports large, smooth leaves and greenish-yellow flowers that appear in spring. These flowers are not as showy as the ones associated with southern magnolias. The tree acquired its name because the immature fruit it bears looks like a cucumber. Cucumber trees do well in rich, well-drained soil in deciduous forests like this one and can grow taller than 100 feet in extreme cases.

The Walks

Normally you *can* judge a book by its cover - that's what a good book cover is for. But not at Ellis Hollow Nature Preserve. From the parking lot you wind through a thick shock of vegetation, your dog unable to see anything but the NYSEG utility lines running overhead. Just when your dog's ears are beginning to droop things change in a big way.

You step into the forest and the feel of this canine hike changes immediately. There is little understory in the mature woodland and you can see that you will be working uphill to the back of the property. To avoid the steepest climbs take the main red-blazed trail in a counter-clockwise direction. this way you hike up a series of natural, step-like ledges. The surface under paw is dirt, often obscured by soft leaf litter.

Just when you think this is a pleasant woodland excursion and nothing more you reach the back of the preserve and start rolling through a series of creek-fed ravines. When you bring your dog back to the trailhead you feel like you have just finished a good rollercoaster ride and want to hop right back on. And you can, by setting off on the smaller, interior yellow-blazed loop.

Trail Sense: A kiosk is at the trailhead once you reach the woods that provides trailmap/brochures and the route is well-blazed.

Dog Friendliness
Dogs are welcome to hike at Ellis Hollow.
Traffic
The trails are maintained for passive visitation - no bikes and horse by permit only. The parking lot only holds one car so don't expect much competition for these trails.
Canine Swimming
The hills are lubricated by several small streams suitable for splashing.
Trail Time
About one hour.

16
Stony Brook
State Park

The Park

A local landowner was the first to look into the Stony Brook gorge and see dollar signs. He built a few conveniences and began charging curious visitors a small admission fee.

In 1883 a railroad was built into Dansville and Stony Brook became a popular summer destination for well-heeled tourists. A high railroad bridge was built across the gorge (the massive stone and concrete footings are still in the gorge so you can see exactly *how* high) that brought guests directly into the resort. The Stony Brook railroad station once stood where the campground office is today.

By the 1920s summer tourists had been passing by Stony Brook for glitzier destinations for years. New York State revived the tired resort by purchasing 250 acres here and creating the state park. Franklin Roosevelt's Civilian Conservation Corps went to work here in the1930s, like they did at so many New York parks, building trails and freshening the park.

Steuben County

Phone Number
- (585) 335-8111

Website
- nysparks.state.ny.us/parks/info.asp?parkID=102

Admission Fee
- Vehicle entrance fee May to November

Park Hours
- Daylight hours

**Nearest Finger Lake
- south of Conesus**

Directions
- *Dansville*; take Route 36 South from I-390, three miles south of town on the left side of the road.

The Walks

As with the Finger Lakes' other gorge parks, Stony Brook connects its Lower Park to the Upper Park with three trails. From the Lower Park the *Gorge Trail* works upstream past three major waterfalls and a fistful of smaller ones. Although you are going from 750 feet in elevation to 1,250 feet your dog won't notice it much until the rim trails. Like other trails constructed through steep gorges this one can be closed for safety reasons in bad weather.

Bonus
Seneca Indians fishing in Stony Brook were familiar
with gas bubbles rising from the water.
In 1882, a local entrepreneur tried to strike oil by
drilling near the bubbles. No oil but the natural gas
was used for lighting and cooking. The gas bubbles can
still be seen in the lower part of the park.

Your climbing begins in earnest when you hike out of the gorge. The *West Rim Trail* uses steps to reach the rim where you won't be rewarded with many jaw-dropping views. This is more a forest hike - and a good one - rather than an excursion to see the gorge.

Trail Sense: A map/brochure is available to take along and there are directional signs at the trailheads.

Dog Friendliness
Dogs are welcome to hike in the Stony Brook gorge but can't play in the playground.

Traffic
Bikes are not permitted on the trails; more folks come for the swimming and playground than to go deep into the gorge on the trails.

Canine Swimming
Your dog can find safe spots to slip in the water to cool off but no major swimming holes, unless the human swimming area is filled with water and not filled with people.

Trail Time
Several hours.

The Gorge Trail *at Stony Brook will put a smile on any dog's face.*

47

17
Sweedler Preserve at Lick Brook

The Park

Cornell math professor Moss Sweedler would occasionally publish under the name "Boo Barkee," Boo being the name of his former dog.

The 120 acres he owned around the gorge at Lick Brook had been in private hands for 200 years when the Finger Lakes Land Trust came calling. It had long been "number one" on the conservation group's "hit list" for protection. Sweedler had always intended to deed Lick Brook to the trust after his death but the story goes he decided to act sooner - by trading a spectacular piece of land that could pass for a state park for a lesser piece of property with a pond where his dogs could swim. Dog owners can relate.

The Walks

You will be taking your dog down to the bottom of a 500-foot gorge and

Tompkins County

Phone Number
- None

Website
- www.fllt.org/protected_lands/protected_lands1.php?id=29

Admission Fee
- None

Park Hours
- Sunrise to sunset

Nearest Finger Lake - south of Cayuga

Directions
- *Ithaca*; take Route 13 South. Turn left on Sandbank Road, just past Buttermilk Falls State Park. At the Y intersection, bear right on Town Line Road; park on the right side of road, just before the bridge.

back up at Lick Brook so don't be lulled into your "stolling" pace by the gentle entrance path of wood chips. It is about a two-mile round trip on the hillside between two gullies and a serious canine hike indeed.

You have your choice of how to attack the gorge and its three major waterfalls. If you prefer a more gradual ascent and don't mind a straight-down descent, take the blue-blazed trail to the floor of the gorge. If you favor a safer climb down with a harder hike up, stay on the white-blazed *Finger Lakes Trail* to the bottom. Either way, your dog is in for a work-out. Take care on the edges of the gorge - they are unprotected but the trail doesn't get that close so it should not be dangerous.

Bonus

Lick Brook has long been a place to see the crow-sized peregrine falcon. The world's fastest bird - over 200 mph in its attack dive - prefers to nest on clifftops like those found here. Peregrines feed almost exclusively on birds such as doves, waterfowl and songbirds, plunging into the wings of its victim to cushion its impact. Perches like those above the 140-foot waterfall give it clear sightlines to a meal.

Trail Sense: There is a trailmap available and the two trails are well-marked. If you cross the Conrail railroad tracks you know you've left the preserve.

Dog Friendliness
Dogs are allowed to hike around Lick Brook.

Traffic
Foot traffic only; its nickname of the "Lost Gorge" gives you the idea it is not a mainstream destination. And you won't find many casual hikers here.

Canine Swimming
Your dog can cool off under the waterfall at the bottom of the gorge but it is an untidy plunge pool.

Trail Time
About one hour.

Expect a weary dog when you cimb out of the Lick Brook gorge.

49

18
Stevenson
Forest Preserve

The Park

After the Revolutionary War the Harvey family left New Jersey for the wilderness of central New York on the Sullivan Trail. Like other veterans coming to claim their lots for compensation

Tompkins County

Phone Number
- None

Website
- www.fllt.org/protected_lands/protected_lands1.php?id=30

Admission Fee
- None

Park Hours
- Sunrise to sunset

**Nearest Finger Lake
- west of Cayuga**

Directions
- *Ithaca*; take Route 13 South to Route 327 North. Turn left on Trumbull Corners Road and the preserve is 1/2 mile on the right, before the stream. Parking is on the roadside.

in the Revolution, they hacked out their land. The Harvey and Stevenson families soon became intertwined by marriage.

Two hundred years later, the last 150 undisturbed, the land came down to Elizabeth Stevenson Bennett through inheritance. She had not visited her 25 acres here until donating it in 1995 to the Finger Lakes Land Trust to form the core of the 83-acre preserve. Your dog won't want to wait that long for his visit.

Bonus
You normally don't want to advocate the scarring of magnificent old trees but you might notice one carving in an old beech tree - "Rex, R.S., 1938."
It was etched there by a grieving ten-year old boy, Dick Stevenson, in memory of his dog.

The Walks

Your canine hike in the stately Stevenson Forest starts smartly in a cool hemlock forest as you climb to meet the white blazes of the *Finger Lakes Trail*. Once there, turn uphill through the hemlocks before transitioning to an oak-beech climax forest at the fallow field opening.

From here the length of your day's outing is up to you. Adjacent to the preserve is the Reiman Woods, a private conservation area managed by the Cayuga Trails Club. Another neighbor is the Treman State Park. You can take your dog on the *Finger Lakes Trail* back and forth for two hours and never notice the time passing in these unhurried woodlands.

Trail Sense: No map at the trailhead but the trails are well-blazed.

Dog Friendliness
Dogs are allowed to hike through the Stevenson Forest.
Traffic
No bikes and no horses; maybe you will see someone on these trails on a sunny weekend.
Canine Swimming
The fast-moving stream near the trailhead provides cool relief for your dog after a long day on the trail.
Trail Time
More than one hour.

"Happiness is dog-shaped."
-Chapman Pincher

19
Connecticut Hill State Wildlife Management Area

The Park

Once called Saxton Hill, Connecticut Hill came by its name honestly. The mountain, at 2.097 feet the highest point in Tompkins County, was part of a 16,000 acre tract acquired in 1800 by the State of Connecticut and owned by the Nutmeg State for parts of the next 50 years. An interesting concept; perhaps the next time New York runs a budget surplus it could buy Mystic Seaport or something...

Farmers who settled here did not last long. A harsh climate and thin soils soon sent them on their way. New York State acquired almost 10,000 acres of the Hill for use as a game refuge in the early 1900s. Since that time, Connecticut Hill has been the site of many experimental programs and studies designed to gain insight into the habits and needs of wildlife species. Today, Connecticut Hill is the largest Wildlife Management Area in New York State, totaling 11,045 acres.

Tompkins County

Phone Number
- (607) 753-3095

Website
- www.dec.ny.gov/out-door/9331.html

Admission Fee
- None

Park Hours
- Sunrise to sunset

**Nearest Finger Lake
- west of Cayuga**

Directions
- *Newfield*; on the north side of Route 13. Take Connecticut Hill Road into the maze of unpaved roads.

The Walks

Most canine hiking in the wilderness on Connecticut Hill is conducted on a leg of the *Finger Lakes Trail (FLT)* that passes through the park. The FLT is a 562.9-mile long footpath that crosses the south end of the Finger Lakes while extending from the Catskills Forest Preserve in the east to the Allegany State Park in the west.

There are two hiking loops that ust the *FLT* as a stem here. the *Bob Cameron Loop* (named for a former caretaker on the property), located to the west

52

Bonus

The State of New York erected an historical marker on
Connecticut Hill in 1938 that read:
"Born here, July 22, 1855, to
Foster Ervay and wife, four
children, know as Ervay
Quadruplets, on exhibition
for several years"
The marker is curious for a couple of things.
First, it gives the lion's share of credit for the multiple
birth to Foster Ervay rather than his wife Lucinda, who
one assumes did most of the heavy lifting here.
In fact, these were the 9th, 10th, 11th and 12th
children for the couple and Lucinda would give birth
twice more.Second, although P.T. Barnum never met a
set of quadruplets he didn't like, it is unlikely that he
exhibited the Ervay quadruplets. According to
family genealogical records, Iva died at the age of
three months on Connecticut Hill and Ina did not
survive her first year either. The remaining quads,
Irvan and Ida both lived into their seventies.

of Tower Road, traverses the top of Connecticut Ridge. You start in a twisting field of young conifers and won't drop down too dramatically in its 2.6-mile course. You may notice open areas near this hike - proposals have been floated to establish wind turbines up on Connecticut Hill.

Experienced canine hikers will love the sporty climbs around Cayuta Creek on the 5.8-mile *Van Lone Hill Loop* (end of a dirt road of CR 6, south of Cayuta Lake). In addition to the well-maintained natural trails, this loop uses old logging roads as well.

Trail Sense: The roads are unmarked, the trailheads are unmarked, the roads are hard to follow - don't bring your dog here as an afterthought. Have a map and a plan. The *Finger Lakes Trail* is blazed in white; the loop trails in orange.

Dog Friendliness
Dogs are welcome across Connecticut Hill.
Traffic
The *Finger Lakes Trail* loops are popular with adventurers in warm weather and snow but certainly not as crowded as less rustic parks.
Canine Swimming
Plenty of streams and ponds; the ponds were built after World War II to attract waterfowl for hunters, Cayuta Creek has some good pools.
Trail Time
A full day possible.

20
Montezuma National Wildlife Refuge

The Park

The name "Montezuma" was first used in 1806 when Dr. Peter Clark named his hilltop home after the Aztec Emperor Montezuma. Eventually the Marsh, the Village, and the Refuge all acquired the name.

The wetlands survived the building of the Erie Canal to its north but the Seneca River was dramatically altered by the expansion of the Cayuga extension to the canal in 1910. The level of the river plunged eight feet and the water drained from the marshes.

In 1937 the Bureau of Biological Survey, which later became the U.S. Fish and Wildlife Service, purchased 6,432 acres of the former marsh and set about building dikes to restore the marsh habitat. In 1938, Montezuma Migratory Bird Refuge was established to provide resting, nesting, and feeding habitat for waterfowl and other migratory birds. Since its opening 320 species of birds have been identified here.

Seneca County

Phone Number
- (315) 568-5987

Website
- www.fws.gov/r5mnwr

Admission Fee
- Donations accepted

Park Hours
- Sunrise to sunset

**Nearest Finger Lake
- north of Cayuga**

Directions
- *Seneca Falls*; From Exit 41 of the New York State Thruway that bisects the refuge go south on Route 414 and east on Route 318 to the main entrance on Route 5/20.

The Walks

One of the reasons often given for keeping dogs off trails in National Parks is that dogs disturb wildlife. So you might be surprised to learn about some of the best lands our federal government maintains where you can hike with your dog - our National Wildlife Refuges.

While the priority of National Wildlife Refuges is to manage lands for the benefit of wildlife, human visitors are welcome in 98 percent of the refuges. And most will welcome your dog in as well. And that is the case at Montezuma.

Bonus

Montezuma was the release site for the world's first bald eagle "hacking" program where young bald eagles were relocated, artificially raised and released back into the wild. The female of the first pair, Agnes, was set free in 1976 and returned to nest in 1980. Several pairs of nesting bald eagles - they are monogamous and mate for life - can be seen here. They build large nests, called eyries, at the top of sturdy tall trees.

Unlike most wildlife refuges you can hike on more than park roads here. In fact, there is no walking on Wildlife Drive.

The marquee dog hike is on the *Esker Brook Nature Trail*, actually a series of three parallel paths that combine into a 1.5-mile loop. Your dog will be trotting along a glacially formed ridge, through a long-gone apple orchard and down to the views across man-made ponds. This is easy going through light woods on natural dirt and gravel footpaths.

For a sensuous open-air excursion, guide your dog around the .75-mile *Oxbow Trail* on wide mown paths in a refuge grassland. The route visits the edge of the water where you can see carp in the stream and canal.

Trail Sense: A park map is available at the visitor contact station.

Dog Friendliness

Dogs are welcome to hike the refuge trails.

Traffic

Foot traffic only.

Canine Swimming

The water here is for the birds, not the dogs.

Trail Time

More than one hour.

Montezuma NWR is bounded by the Cayuga-Seneca Barge Canal and you can watch boat traffic float by from the **Oxbow** *Trail.*

21
Camillus Forest Unique Area

The Park

Camillus, named for Marcus Furius Camillus, a Roman general and dictator, sprung up when early settler William Lindsey discovered the first plaster beds in the United States here in 1792. Vast areas of forest were cleared for cropland and pastureland for sheep to graze.

In 1926, the property was bought by New York State as a farm colony for disabled young men. The Syracuse State School farm raised livestock, eggs, milk and grains to supply other state facilities and state prisons. Farm residents were trained to become self-sufficient.

In 1966, a fire destroyed three large barns. In 1971, the last crops were planted by the State School, although some land was rented for agriculture through 1996. The State was ready to sell the land to a developer but when plans were revealed to harvest a rare, 40-acre stand of old growth forest on the 700-foot hilltop they reversed the deal and protected this property.

Onandaga County

Phone Number
- None

Website
- www.dec.ny.gov/lands/28312.html

Admission Fee
- None

Park Hours
- Sunrise to sunset

Nearest Finger Lake - north of Otisco

Directions
- *Amboy*; From Route 5, exit north onto Newport Road away from town. Turn right onto Devoe Road and right again onto Thompson Road after crossing the canal. Continue to the end and turn left on Warners Road. The park is up the hill on the left.

The Walks

Most of the time when you go out hiking with your dog you are going for a walk in the woods, Here you hike with your dog *to* the woods. That hike requires some purchase - you will be climbing on a sometimes-rutted, maybe muddy, maybe overgrown farm road. You are compensated by long, unfettered views to the south and to the east to Onandaga Lake.

Bonus
You don't get a chance to hike with your dog through many old-growth forests like this one.
Tree surveys have determined that many of the arboreal giants are at least 150 years old. Some of the 100-footers are over 200 years old and one was dated with annual growth rings at 285 years old - growing happily here long before European settlers arrived.

You'll see the Camillus Forest in the distance as you hike, and when you enter your dog will be trotting in the prettiest slice of forest in the Finger Lakes. Probably five of every six trees is a sugar maple, its trunk branchless until high in the canopy. There is little understory and long views in the darkish woodland. The trail slides around and over little hillocks on paw-friendly soft dirt paths until your dog returns to the grassy trail back to parking lot.

It is wide open spaces for your dog in the 355-acre park until he reaches the Camillus Forest.

Trail Sense: There is no map - follow the farm road out of the parking lot. There is one critical right turn through a gate and no markings until a post where the trail forks just before the forest that marks the beginning through the forest. The trail is blazed once you reach the trees.

Dog Friendliness
Dogs are allowed to hike the trail to Camillus Forest.
Traffic
This is a lightly used park.
Canine Swimming
None; you cross one shallow seasonal creek that is conveniently situated half-way up the hill to refresh your dog coming and returning.
Trail Time
About one hour.

22
Harriet Hollister Spencer State Recreation Area

The Park

This wilderness high above Honeoye Lake resembles little the world of its benefactor, Harriet Hollister Spencer. Mrs. Spencer was born in 1887, the daughter of Granger A. Hollister, whose grandfather founded the Hollister Lumber Co. in Rochester in 1832. As an adult she was a rose expert and charter member of the Rochester Garden Club. She designed the "Garden of Fragrance" at the Rochester Museum and Science Center and was awarded the Garden Club of America Rose Medal Award in 1959. Mrs. Spencer was an authority on glass, silver and lace and she served as a consultant to the Memorial Art Gallery. At her request, following her death the family gave to the people of New York State 679 acres of land here. The only touch of civilization added by the State to the Harriet Hollister Spencer State Memorial Recreation Area is a small pavilion. Not a cultivated rose in sight.

Ontario County

Phone Number
- (585) 335-8111

Website
- nysparks.state.ny.us/parks/info.asp?parkID=98

Admission Fee
- None

Park Hours
- Daylight hours

**Nearest Finger Lake
- west of Honeoye**

Directions
- *Honeoye*; from Route 20A west of the village take Route 37 South. When the road turns to gravel in about five miles you are on Canadice Hill Road. the parking area is up the hill on the left.

The Walks

The recreation area sports one of the largest trail systems in the Finger Lakes - more than 16 miles. These trails were really designed for cross-country skiers who often find snow here when the surrounding area is bare. You do get to sample a taste of the Spencer trails before you decide to tackle the bulk of the system. At the entrance parking lot is the 1.9-mile *Big Oak/Bear Cub Loop*. If your dog takes a liking to the cool forest and occasional steep stretches then

Bonus

Who is Todd Ewers and why is this one of his favorite places? The former isn't really important and the latter is obvious. The open view of Honeoye Lake will be your most memorable reminder of a canine hike here. No wonder Todd liked the bench on this spot.

drive down the entrance road and really start to get into it.

The trails are actually quite manageable for hikers, broken into chunks of between one and two miles. If you can find a ski map you can determine the amount of difficulty to expect on the hike. Your dog will do some panting but nothing extreme.

Trail Sense: A park map is available and quite handy since the trails can be unreliably blazed, especially single tracks in places.

Dog Friendliness
Dogs are allowed throughout the park.
Traffic
Watch out for mountain bikers; the trails attract only hardcore hikers until the leaves change color in the fall.
Canine Swimming
Come for the hiking, not the swimming.
Trail Time
Several hours of trail time are available.

"The greatest pleasure of a dog is that you may make a fool of yourself with him, and not only will he not scold you, but will make a fool of himself too."
- Samuel Butler

23

Arnot Teaching and Research Forest

The Park

John Arnot walked to this area from Boston in 1827 and bought six square miles of land. He made his fortune by logging the land and then founded a bank, the Chemung Canal Trust Company.

Joseph Rodbourn and his brother James were teamsters from Erin who built the infamous Confederate prisoner camp at Elmira during the Civil War. They took their considerable profit and bought timber stands here. They made a fortune by logging the land and invested in more timber down in Tidewater Virginia.

The economy of the 1890s soured and the Rodbourns were forced to mortgage their land with Arnot's bank. In 1910 they foreclosed. The land was sold to the Matthias H. Arnot Estate and 1,641 acres were donated to Cornell in 1927. Total acreage is now over 4,000 and has been managed as second hand timber since 1984.

The Walks

This is not a forest laced with must-

Tompkins County

Phone Number
- (607) 589-6076

Website
- www.dnr.cornell.edu/arnot/

Admission Fee
- None

Park Hours
- Sunrise to 5:30 p.m. during hunting season; open at 9:00 a.m. otherwise

**Nearest Finger Lake
- southwest of Cayuga**

Directions
- *Van Etten*; from Route 13, approximately 4 miles west of the intersection of Routes 13, 34, and 96, turn left at Trumbulls Corners Road just before the Newfield Post Office. Turn right on Main Street at the "T". Take the first left onto VanKirk Road. Go 4 miles, bear to the left at the Irish Hill Road intersection and continue to the forest entrance road past the lodge on the right.

do hiking trails but don't let that keep you from bringing your dog to experience Arnot. Much of your canine hiking will be on old forest roads and as you push away from the maple syrup barn at the parking lot you will quickly adopt the sense of walking down a country lane. The woods are airy and since Cornell

Bonus

While hiking with your dog you may chance to see what seems like a wild goat. The forest has hosted the Goats In Woods Project since 1997. The idea is that goat herds may be brought off the pastureland to browse Northeast woodlands and control bushes and undesired tree species like striped maple and beech. This would reduce the need to treat forest areas with pesticides and help woodlot owners with inexpensive woody plant control.

maintains some open space in the forest this is one of the best places for a fall foliage hike with your dog.

The hard-packed dirt roads are wide enough to allow vehicles to pass each other so there is plenty of room for a pack of dogs. The terrain is hilly but not oppressively so. Like most roads these lead some place and

There is plenty of room for your dog to stretch out on the airy Arnot Forest road trails.

don't loop so you are on your own in planning your approach to the forest.

Trail Sense: The forest is marked with a grid system that locates 37 individual "lots". Corners of the lots are marked by red painted posts with metal tags that identify the corner. A map can be printed off the website to take with you.

Dog Friendliness
Dogs are welcome to hike these forest trails.

Traffic
Since these are active forest roads you can expect just about anything but most of the time you will be alone with your dog here.

Canine Swimming
Banfield Creek is more for splashing; depending on how far you hike your dog may encounter one of the ten ponds int he forest.

Trail Time
Many hours possible.

24
Elizabeth Mulholland Wildflower Preserve

The Park

Robert H. Treman gave the people the land around lower Six Mile Creek as a public playgound. The City of Ithaca, meanwhile, uses the water in the creek to provide some four million gallons of drinking water daily.

The first dam built by the City here was the 36-foot Six Mile Creek Dam in 1903. Below it four years later they put up the Van Natta Dam. Finally, in 1911 came the Potters Fall Dam with a height of 75 feet and a length of 220 feet, holding back water in the Ithaca Reservoir. You will still see abandoned water pipes here and there on this hike.

Elizabeth Burdick Mulholland was a passionate quilter, tireless advocate for nature preservation and benefactor to the community who died in 2004 at the age of 89.

Tompkins County

Phone Number
- None

Website
- None

Admission Fee
- None

Park Hours
- Sunrise to sunset

**Nearest Finger Lake
- southeast of Cayuga**

Directions
- *Ithaca*; from Route 79 in town heading east, take a right on Giles Street. Continue down the hill to the preserve parking lot at the bottom on the right, before the creek.

The Walks

Unlike the area's other gorges that required an army of workers to construct stone paths along the water, the trails along Six Mile Creek evolved more naturally. It is a tamer walk and although you are close to downtown Ithaca your dog will find the wooded creekside quiet and leafy.

The wildflower preserve is roughly at the center of the Six Mile Creek trail system and most trail users head upstream from this point. The wildflower walk follows the creek upstream, then loops back through the woods to the parking lot.

Bonus
Led by an onslaught of white and red trillium the wildflower preserve puts on its best show in May. Dutchmen's breeches, hepatica, bloodroot, white and red baneberries, blue and black cohosh, mayapple, and violets make up a strong supporting cast.

Staying with the stream and moving on, the well-worn dirt path hugs the north shoreline of as it skirts a lake and passes plenty of cascading water, both natural and man-made. The trail ends at the Ithaca Reservoir that is off-limits to the public. The round-trip will cover more than four miles.

Trail Sense: The trails are unmarked and you are certain to take one or two missteps here - even following your dog's nose.

Dog Friendliness
Dogs are allowed to explore the shale rock gorge.

Traffic
No bikes allowed but plenty of traffic, both human and canine.

Canine Swimming
Hard as it may be, try and keep your dog out of Ithaca's drinking water supply.

Trail Time
More than one hour.

25
Ted Markham Nature Center

The Park

During October of 1963 a small brush fire got out of control and was soon rushing up the hillside south of Bath. Quickly 300 acres were aflame. Hundreds of firefighters, volunteers and State forest rangers battled this stubborn blaze for more than three days. On the second day the conflagration measured 1 mile wide by 4 miles in circumference. A fixed-wing airplane flew over, dumping a reported 4,000 gallons of water on the fire. From the ashes would grow Mossy Bank Park after the Village of Bath appropriated $1,700 to build a municipal recreation area.

Ted Markham was the original chairperson of the Mossy Bank park committee and has served in a variety of capacities since. In May 2007 the park was re-named in his honor.

Steuben County

Phone Number
- None

Website
- None

Admission Fee
- None

Park Hours
- 10:00 a.m - 10:00 p.m.

**Nearest Finger Lake
- southwest of Keuka**

Directions
- *Bath*; south of the village. Take I-86 Exit 39 to Route 415 North into town. Turn left on Cameron Street and left on Mossy Bank Park Road to the park at the end.

The Walks

As you pull into the small circular drive around the park this seems like a place for dogs - a bit rough around the edges; the trash cans are riddled with bullet holes, for instance. It doesn't prepare you for the first-rate quality of these trails.

There are a half-dozen short, interconnecting pahways. The one you won't want to miss is the yellow-blazed trail that loops across the eastern part of the park. Most of your dog's hiking is fairly level on this mountaintop although this path does drop down the hill a bit. You will be traveling through a dark hemlock forest where the only understory is the fallen remains of the trees

Bonus
Situated atop Sharps Hill, the park is best known
for the panoramic view from its Overlook.
Spread before you are the Village of Bath,
the Cohocton River and the valley beyond.
Come for the view and stay for the hiking.

*Your dog will not find a better view in the Finger Lakes
than the one from the overlook on Sharps Hill.*

that went before. Like all the trails in the park, your dog will be enjoying wide,
soft footpaths.

Trail Sense: An accurate mapboard is at the trailhead and the trails are
well-blazed.

Dog Friendliness
Dogs are welcome in the park and picnic areas.
Traffic
Foot traffic only on the hiking trails.
Canine Swimming
None.
Trail Time
About an hour.

26
Naples
"Gullies"

The Park

During its early years, the Naples Valley was thought to be anything but a prosperous area. Once the site of an ancient Seneca Indian Nation named "Nundawao," Naples was considered among the least desirable territories for sale due to its barren and mountainous territory. The first settlers here purchased the land for a mere 12 cents per acre.

The steep hills surrounding the town are chock full of waterfalls. This trio close to Naples will lure adventurous canine hikers who love the hydrospectaculars.

The Walks

Many of the waterfalls in the Finger Lakes are best reached by hiking directly in the streambed. This can intimidate some dogs but if you want to introduce your dog to rock scrambling in creeks these gullies provide a benign introduction to the art.

Grimes Glen: The easiest of the three to reach, via a bouncy dirt trail on the left side of the creek, there are three waterfalls in the glen. Your dog can only hike to two, unless he knows how to climb a rope. If your dog balks at crossing the bridge, and it looks like it might fall down anytime, you can hike straight up the shallow creek.

Tannery Creek: By far the least visited of the three Naples gullies, maybe because there is no path at all. Start your hike by scampering down a short embankment behind the maintenance shed and begin forging ahead through the

Yates County
Phone Number - None
Website - None
Admission Fee - None
Park Hours - Sunrise to sunset
Nearest Finger Lake - south of Canandaigua
Directions - *Conklin Gully*; northeast of town on Parrish Hill Road off Route 245, *Grimes Glen*; in town at end of Vine Street off Route 21, *Tannery Falls*; in town at end of Tannery Road from Route 21 and then Route 54.

Bonus

In 1882, Dana Luther, a Naples biologist, discovered the fossil of one of the oldest trees in the world at Grimes Glen. The tree, which had a trunk eighteen feet in diameter, is believed to be from the Devonian Period - over 350 million years ago. "The Naples Tree" is currently on display in the New York State Museum in Albany.

shallow water. There are a series of cascades before your reach the big falls.

Conklin Gully: There are a couple of things you can do with your dog here. Hiking up the streambed will bring you shortly to a cascading waterfall with a good plunge pool. While others may climb on this will probably be the end of your in-stream adventure with a dog. On the north side of the stream you can pick up an unmarked dirt trail that begins and ends with a steep climb through the pines. Your destination is the top of Angel Falls and a glimpse of its 120-foot drop. This is not a trail for an untrained or boisterous dog - the gorge is unfenced and the trail tickles the cliff edges.

Trail Sense: There are no markings on any trail and no signs.

Dog Friendliness
Dogs are welcome to explore these gullies.
Traffic
Grimes and Conklin can get crowded on a hot summer weekend.
Canine Swimming
Almost constantly.
Trail Time
More than one hour.

Your dog will find this ceremonial rock path in Grimes Glen.

27
Dorothy McIlroy
Bird Sanctuary

The Park

The preserve is named for Dorothy McIlroy, a dedicated birder who helped create the Cornell Laboratory of Ornithology. Today the lab is the repository of the world's greatest collection of bird sounds, with more than 160,000 on file.

After her death in 1999 at the age of 91, her children gave money to the Finger Lakes Land Trust to establish a preserve in her memory. The trustees were able to purchase 128 acres at the outlet of Lake Como and open the sanctuary in 2003. Additional donations have swelled the protected acreage to 156.

The Walks

The park is located on a high plateau south of Skaneateles Lake in a spot where a ridge to the west knocks down the prevailing winds. The result is an environment colder than the surrounding area where a rich shrub fen has graded into a peat swamp. For your dog, this means cool shade on her hike from the dark hemlocks above that dominate the preserve and a soft surface below to trot on.

A narrow ribbon of dirt snakes through this boreal swamp forest, stopping for looks out across the wetlands. You can't find a better half-hour canine hike in the Finger Lakes.

Trail Sense: No maps but the trail is obvious and it is blazed in yellow.

Cayuga County
Phone Number - None
Website - www.fllt.org/protected_ lands/protected_lands1. php?id=28
Admission Fee - None
Park Hours - Sunrise to sunset
Nearest Finger Lake - south of Skaneateles
Directions - *Summerhill*; From Route 281 go west on Route 90 for 5 miles to Lake Como Road and turn right. Continue for about 2 miles past the cluster of houses to Fire Lane A. Make a right onto lane to find the parking area on the right.

Bonus

So many hemlocks have started to die that the forest of the sanctuary has begun to resemble a hemlock junkyard. The beloved shade trees are being killed by a tiny, aphid-like creature, the hemlock woolly adelgid. The insect first appeared in the eastern United States in Roanoke, Virginia, in the 1950s. It stayed around there until the late 1980s, when it started migrating north. The first evidence that a hemlock is infested with adelgids is that it doesn't get much annual growth. It starts to lose its needles, its crown thins, and it looks gray as the killers devour the starch in its needles and twigs. A mature hemlock will succumb in seven to ten years. Scientists have tried to introduce beetles as a natural control andinsecticide in the soil around healthy hemlocks but there is a very realpossibility that all hemlocks may someday disappear.

Dog Friendliness

Dogs are allowed to trot these trails.

Traffic

Foot traffic only, a little of that.

Canine Swimming

There is no real swimming for your dog near the headwaters of Fall Creek.

Trail Time

Less than one hour.

28
Ontario Pathways

The Park

The Canandaigua and Corning Railroad Company was incorporated by a special act of the New York Legislature on May 14, 1845 to build between the two points named. On March 8, 1850 the legislature was at it again and passed another special act authorizing the Canandaigua & Corning to change its name to the Canandaigua & Elmira and connect with the Chemung RR. Meanwhile, they had yet to run a train, waiting for their initial order of their "Great Western" locomotive. On September 14, 1852, the was renamed the Canandaigua and Elmira Railroad Company. In 1886 the line, now including a branch from Stanley to Canandaigua, was consolidated into the Elmira and Lake Ontario Railroad

Ontario County

Phone Number
- 585-234-7722

Website
- www.ontariopathways.org

Admission Fee
- None

Park Hours
- Daylight hours

**Nearest Finger Lake
- northeast of Canandaigua**

Directions
- *Canandaigua*; at the Ontario County Fairgrounds on Route 10 or Ontario Street
Phelps; on Route 96, west of town.

Company that lasted for 70 years until swallowed by the Northern Central. All that history was washed away in a week when Hurricane Agnes roared through in 1972 scattering tracks, displacing bridges and damging the railroad bed. The old line here was never rebuilt. In 1994 the rail was sold for scrap and the right-of-way was sold to Ontario Pathways.

The Walks

The Ontario Pathways volunteers have cleared 23 miles of trail and have opened 19 of them in a wedge from Phelps in the north to Stanley in the south to Canandaigua in the west. The paths have been cleared to a width of 12 feet although with the lush vegetation along the way the conduit can seem narrower. Your dog would probably prefer the Stanley-to-Phelps leg that is primarily

Bonus
Every October the trail is the site for
The Great Pumpkin Walk where many hundreds of
skillfully carved jack-o-lanterns line the path for about
a half-mile. The scary strut is at the Canandaigua
terminus, free parking is at the Ontario County
Fairgrounds on County Road 10.
Your dog is not allowed on this hike but would
probably be too scared anyway.

carved out of grass and natural surfaces. A popular out-and-back on this leg is from the northern terminus down to Double Drop Falls on Flint Creek and back. A natural turn-around point is where the trail switches to roadways just before Orleans.

The Canandaigua-to-Stanley leg covers 11 miles on hard-packed dirt and cinders. The terrain is all flat and easy through a mix of wooded canopy and open fields.

Trail Sense: There are descriptive map brochures available from kiosks at either end of the trail.

Dog Friendliness
Leashed dogs are welcome on the trail.

Traffic
You'll see just about any mode of transportation that isn't motorized.

Canine Swimming
Flint Creek can flow deep enough for a lap or two, especially in the spring.

Trail Time
Many hours possible.

*"No one appreciates the very special genius
of your conversation as a dog does."*
-Christopher Morley

29

Watkin Glens State Park

The Park

In 1856 Morvalden Ells, a newspaperman, left Elmira to buy the Watkins *Republican*. He saw the "Big Gully" here with a promoter's eye. Ells looked at wooden bridges and walkways built for workers to reach a mill and obtained permission to charge public an admission to see what the millers saw every day on their way to work.

Watkins Glen opened officially as a tourist mecca on July 4, 1863. It probably wasn't front page news - Union forces had stopped the Rebel advance at Gettysburg and the town of Vicksburg, Mississippi surrendered to Ulysses S. Grant that same day in the Civil War. Still, the gorge would quickly become the most famous of all the Finger Lakes attractions.

Ells quit his job to run his concession full time. He gave all 19 waterfalls fanciful names and improved access. Over the years the property passed through many private hands until 1906 when the State bought the gorge for $46,512.

Schuyler County

Phone Number
- (607) 535-4511

Website
- nysparks.state.ny.us/parks/info.asp?parkID=105

Admission Fee
- Vehicle entrance fee May to November

Park Hours
- Daylight hours

Nearest Finger Lake
- south shore of Seneca

Directions
- *Watkins Glen*; in town on Franklin Street (Route 14). To reach the Upper Park, with more parking and where your dog can hike, take Route 14 North three blocks to Route 409 (Steuben Street) and stay on Route 409 when it becomes Station Road. The park is on the left. For the South Entrance take Route 329 off Franklin Street on the south side of Glen Creek.

What you see today in New York's best example of a swishing pothole gorge is completely different than existed 100 years ago. The Great Hurricane of 1935 washed away concrete walks and iron railings to be replaced by more natural stonework.

Bonus
Over Labor Day 1933, Watkins Glen captured the attention of a Depression-weary nation. Some 350,000 people, including 100,000 over Labor Day weekend, visited the park to gape across the gorge at a seven-point buck stranded on a rocky ledge 180 feet above the stream. It was assumed the buck had been chased to his precarious perch by dogs and was clearly injured on his flank. For 11 days the deer remained stranded. With the eyes of America on them, apparently no idea was rejected by park officials to lure the buck across a plank bridge that had been lowered to the ledge. They tried to lure him across with stuffed deer. They summoned an Indian chief to channel good thoughts. Nothing worked. Finally, the buck saved itself. Gently urged by two wardens it walked unassisted to a spot where the ledge sloped least steeply to the gorge's bottom. As some experts had predicted it would do when it injury was mended, it braced its forelegs, slid smoothly down the 35-foot cliff, loped easily up the other side and out of the national spotlight.

The Walks

Your dog is not allowed to experience the *Gorge Trail* so his experience here will be on the rim trail. The *Indian Trail* on the north rim serves up the best look at the gorge from Overlook Point but there are long stretches with no views. The trail runs moderately down the hillside in a wooded corridor.

The *South Rim Trail* is a segment of the *Finger Lakes Trail* and is your route of choice from the award-winning campground. There isn't much for your dog to see on this side but it is a good ramble through the woods. You can also connect here to the *Queen Catharine Marsh Loop* for several hours of canine hiking through town and around the wetlands of the Seneca Lake Inlet. Each rim trail is about one mile in length and gains almost 500 feet in elevation.

Trail Sense: Just follow the gorge.

Dog Friendliness

Dogs are allowed in the park and in the campground but not on the *Gorge Trail* or in the swimming pool.

Traffic

Not as much on the rims; foot traffic only.

Canine Swimming

None

Trail Time

More than one possible.

30
Erie Canal Park

The Park

As early as 1809 DeWitt Clinton had been appointed one of seven commissioners to examine and survey a route for a canal from the Hudson River to the Great Lakes. Months after he was elected Governor in 1817, on July 4, Clinton turned the first shovelful of dirt for the Erie Canal, of which he was its greatest champion.

Eight years later, hand dug by farmers and immigrant workers, the 363-mile long waterway linking the Atlantic seaboard and the American interior. The Erie Canal, the county's first heroic engineering marvel, quickly became the world's most successful and famous canal.

The original canal was gradually expanded to 70 feet wide and seven feet deep but its usefulness in the railroad age was waning. By 1922 the canal here was dry and abandoned. In 1972 the township purchased a seven-mile stretch from New York State and volunteers began an energetic campaign of cleaning the canal bed, building infrastructure and filling the canal once again.

Onandaga

Phone Number
- None

Website
- www.eriecanalcamillus.com

Admission Fee
- None

Park Hours
- Sunrise to sunset

**Nearest Finger Lake
- north of Otisco**

Directions
- *Camillus*; From Route 5, exit north onto Newport Road away from town. Turn right onto Devoe Road and cross the canal. Parking lots are on either side of the road.

The Walks

Land on either side of the canal has been cleared to provide hiking trails along a four-mile stretch of the enlarged Erie Canal route in Camillus. The park is centrally located so you can hike an approximately four-mile loop with your dog on either side of Devoe Road. Most canine hikers will opt for the *East Side* trails that end impressively at the imposing piers and abutments

Bonus

John Sims operated a provisions store on Warners Road where it crosses the canal in 1856.
He did well enough to eventually sell out and move his family of seven children to Belle Isle. The original building stood until it burned in a fire in 1963. Volunteers built a replica of the Sims Store to serve as park headquarters on Devoe Road. The first floor retains the feel of a 19th century general store and the upstairs rooms serve as a museum of canal history. Behind the Sims Store the *Clinton Ditch Trail* runs along portions of the original Erie Canal.

of the Old Erie Canal Aqueduct that carried water in a wooden trough over the Nine Mile Creek. It took three years to build the aqueduct in 1839 and it is being restored today. The Nine-Mile Creek, by the way, is an excellent canoe trail to paddle with your dog.

This is all easy trotting for your dog with plenty of shade. There are also a couple of side trails to extend your hiking day around the Erie Canal.

Thanks to volunteers, when you step onto trails at the Erie Canal Park you are stepping back into the 19th century.

Trail Sense: There is a map brochure and signs to get you started.

Dog Friendliness
The Canal Park is the only park in Camillus that welcomes dogs.

Traffic
Bikes are allowed on the main trail but not the side walking paths. Since a circumnavigation of the canal requires at least an hour you won't get as many casual strollers as you might on a similarly pretty canine hike.

Canine Swimming
Your dog can slip into the canal for a refreshing swim.

Trail Time
More than one hour.

31

Bear Swamp State Forest

The Park

After the Revolutionary War, veterans were given land here as payment for their service to the cause. Over the next 100 years families settled and cleared away most of the forests. The thin, glacial soils slowly tired, however, and during the Great Depression many farms failed and were abandoned.

New York State acquired the property in the headwaters of Skaneateles Lake in 1931 and began planting red pine and Norway spruce around Bear Swamp, which was more than three-quarters pastureland by this time. You will see the results of these efforts when you visit the 3,316-acre state forest today.

The Walks

Bear Swamp Forest is best known for its elaborate 13-mile Nordic ski trail system. So it is a fine place to ski and snowshoe with your dog but when the snows melt away don't forget about Bear Swamp Forest for a big day of canine hiking.

The first thing your dog will notice upon entering the forest is the fragrant presence of the spruce plantations. The next is the natural feel the trails have - the surface is paw-friendly smooth dirt and the paths swing to and fro rather than moving down old logging roads (although there are some of those too) as is often encountered in state forests.

Grab a trail map before your dog's outing to maximize your enjoyment of the reforested Bear Swamp. A maze of red, blue and yellow-numbered trails

Cayuga County

Phone Number
- (607) 753-3095

Website
- www.stateparks.com/bear_swamp.html

Admission Fee
- None

Park Hours
- Sunrise to sunset

**Nearest Finger Lake
- southwest of Skaneateles**

Directions
- *Sempronius*; From Route 41A take Iowa Road east in town to Bear Swamp Road (unpaved) on the left. Travel north on Bear Swamp Road, looking for parking areas.

Bonus
The Defense Meteorological Satellite Program began putting satellites in orbit in 1965 with sensors sensitive enough to record light from sources on the ground. To date 43 such satellites have been deployed with four currently in operation. Analysis of data from these eyes in the sky have revealed that the darkest spot in Cayuga County is in the Bear Swamp State Forest adjacent to Skaneateles Lake.

allow you to craft any length of canine hike that suits your dog. Although you will be hiking nearly 1,000 feet about Skaneateles Lake (there are places on the trail where the lake is visible) and can actually pass the high point of Cayuga County (1860 feet, along *Trail 4*) there are no violent climbs along the trail system. All your dog's efforts at Bear Swamp will be shaded.

At the edge of the forest your dog can soak in views of the wetlands that lubricate Bear Swamp State Forest.

Trail Sense: There are no maps or park information on site. In fact there are no signs identifying the woodland as the Bear Swamp State Forest. Trailheads are framed by large boulders or posts and the trails are marked by circular shields but without a map they are of minimal value so find a map before you go.

Dog Friendliness
Dogs are allowed to hike throughout the forest.
Traffic
Mountain bikes are popular here but no motorized vehicles; often the trails will be yours to enjoy alone with your dog.
Canine Swimming
The occasional stream is mostly for splashing - after hours on the trail your dog may be wanting more.
Trail Time
Several hours available.

32

Fishers Park

The Park

The town of Victor had been settled for a quarter-century when Charles Fisher arrived to clear land in the northwest part of the village. The first Victor school had opened a year earlier. Fisher harvested lumber and sold cleared land to new settlers. Later generations added fruit to the family enterprise.

In 2001, part of the original Fisher homestead was dedicated as a public park with a donation from J. Sheldon Fisher and the trail system became part of Victor Hiking Trails, Inc. In September of 1991 a group of energetic volunteers formed that organization to promote development of footpaths in and around the town of Victor. They have been obtaining funds, building and maintaining trails ever since. They currently oversee over 20 miles of trail.

Ontario County

Phone Number
- None

Website
- www.victorhikingtrails.org

Admission Fee
- None

Park Hours
- Sunrise to sunset

**Nearest Finger Lake
- northwest of Canandaigua**

Directions
- *Fishers*; driving west out of Victor on West Main Street, Route 96, turn left on Route 42. The park is on the left, just past Wangum Road.

The Walks

Your canine hike here does not begin with a bang but a squish. You will gingerly lead your dog across the Irondequoit Creek and through the valley floor on a carpet of rocks. But soon you are moving uphill into the heart of a clean, airy woodland and your dog's ears will perk up considerably.

Once on the ridge, dirt trails lead in both directions and the trail system evolves through a series of short, interconnecting paths. You can cobble together a three-mile canine hike here, mostly a walk in the woods. Your best bet is to start by heading west to flavor you dog's hiking day with some open, rolling pastureland.

Bonus
Also in the tiny hamlet of Fishers you can see the cobblestone Railroad Pump house, built in 1845 for the Auburn and Rochester railroad – the second oldest surviving railroad structure in the country.
J. Sheldon Fisher was instrumental in saving the distinctive pump house back in the 1930s, the first act of historical preservation in Victor.

Nearby you can access the *Auburn Trail*, a pathway that is narrower and a bit wilder than the usual rail-to-trail project. Hiking east you will reach Lehigh Crossing Park, added to Victor Hiking Trails in 2001, where it crosses the *Lehigh Trail*, another rail-turned trail. Who knows how far you can hike with your dog in Victor?

Trail Sense: There are no maps on site but you can print one off the website. Bring one if you can, it will greatly enhance your hiking across Fishers Park's many trail segments.

Dog Friendliness
Dogs are welcome to trot these trails.

Traffic
This little urban natural area attracts plenty of trail users from joggers to dogwalkers.

Canine Swimming
Irondequoit Creek pools deep enough for limited canine aquatics, especially at the east end of the parking lot.

Trail Time
More than one hour.

33

Ontario County Park at Gannett Hill

The Park

Gannett Hill in the Bristol Hills is the ancestral home of Frank E. Gannett, who was born on this mountain in 1876. At the age of 30 he became partners in his first newspaper, the Elmira *Gazette*. Six years later, in 1912, he purchased the Ithaca *Journal*.

His expanding Finger Lakes media empire shifted to Rochester in 1918. Gannett purchased his first radio station, WHEC, in 1932. He ran for the Republican presidential nomination in 1940 but his bid was derailed by Wendell Wilkie who took the drubbing by Franklin Roosevelt instead.

Gannett died in 1957 when his newspaper conglomerate was still regional - it would later become the nation's second largest newspaper company with *USA Today* as its flagship. Ontario County developed this recreational park at the highpoint in the county - 2,256 feet.

Ontario County
Phone Number - (585) 374-6250
Website - www.co.ontario.ny.us/pub- lic_works/gannett.html
Admission Fee - None
Park Hours - 9:00 a.m. to 9:00 p.m.
Nearest Finger Lake - west of Canandaigua
Directions - *Bristol Springs*; From Route 64 north of town take West Gannett Hill Road up the mountain to a T-interscetion. Turn right to the park.

The Walks

A hodgepodge of paths for hikers and bikers have sprouted on Gannett Hill. It is actually possible to parse together a 1.5-mile canine hike that loops the park. Most trail users will, however, use the main park road and one of numerous spurs to craft their hiking day with the dog.

The hiking trails are narrow, natural surface affairs with plenty of ups and downs while moving around the mountaintop. The highlight will come at the Look Out Area with long, open views of the surrounding Bristol Hills. You

Bonus

Also on Gannett Hill is the C.K. Mees Observatory, located on the grounds of the former summer estate of Frank Gannett. He left the property to the University of Rochester for use as a star-gazing laboratory.

C. E. Kenneth Mees (1882-1960) was a longtime director of research at Eastman Kodak who performed pioneering work in the development of sensitive photographic emulsions for use in astronomy.

Free guided tours are usually offered by students on summer weekends. To reach the estate, turn left on Gannett Hill where you turned right to each the park.

can also set out for a longer adventure with your dog on the *Finger Lakes Trail* or the yellow-blazed bike loop.

Trail Sense: A park map can be obtained from the sentry post at the park entrance and the trails are well-marked.

Dog Friendliness
Dogs are allowed on the trails and in the campground.

Traffic
Foot traffic and mountain bikes on the trails but is seldom heavy.

Canine Swimming
There is easy access to the fishing pond in the center of the park when no anglers are around.

Trail Time
More than one hour.

34
Bare Hill
Unique Area

The Park

Each year Seneca leaders would meet on the hill they called Genundowa to thank Mother Earth for her bounty. A large bonfire would be constructed on the open expanses of Bare Hill and coordinating smaller fires would be lit around the lake in a gesture of Seneca unity. The Genundowa Festival of Lights is celebrated each year on Labor Day Saturday.

The Walks

Bare Hill is not bare, not completely anyway. There are trees and bushes about but your dog will enjoy a romp through mostly open terrain around the summit on wide grass and gravel paths. Bare Hill covers more than a thousand acres and its prime attraction to canine hikers is the view of Canandaigua Lake. The summit tops off at 1540 feet above sea level, more than 850 feet above lake level.

Yates County

Phone Number
- None

Website
- None

Admission Fee
- None

Park Hours
- Sunrise to sunset

Nearest Finger Lake
- east shore of Canandaigua

Directions
- *Middlesex*; north of town via Route 364. From Route 5/20 east of Canandaigua go south on Route 364. Turn right on Town Line Road towards the lake and left on Bare Hill Road. Make a right on Van Epps Road (unpaved) to the park where the road deadends.

Two trails separate at the trailhead and lead uphill, not severely. The favored path is to your left that extends to Council Rock, the large boulder at the center of Seneca celebrations. You will reach the top of the hill in less than one mile before retracing your steps or picking up another parallel trail. For additional trail time on Bare Hill you can sample the lower path. It also deadends but serves up views of the lake as well.

Bonus
Why is Bare Hill bare? According to Seneca tradition, because of a big snake. There are several varying translations and versions of how the monstrous serpent came to be but the legends of its demise are consistent. Only a young warrior and maiden came to escape its wrath and learned that the serpent could be slain with a poison dart under its scales. This they did and the great snake, in its death throes, slid down the mountain slashing away the trees with its tail as it perished. With every tortured motion the serpent disgorged a human head from its victims and they rolled down the hill around the lake, where the round stones are known today as Indian heads.

Trail Sense: A kiosk is at the trailhead that may or may not have a map posted. Nothing is marked on the trail but poking around a bit will take you across all the trails on Bare Hill.

Dog Friendliness
Dogs are welcome to hike on Bare Hill.
Traffic
Bikes can also use the trails but this is not a crowded trail system.
Canine Swimming
A small pond fills the bill nicely.
Trail Time
About one hour.

35
Six Nations Trail System

The Park

Beginning in the 1930s, New York State purchased more than 12,000 acres of land west of Watkins Glen for timber prodcution, recreational use, watershed protection, and wildlife habitat. When President Franklin Roosevelt put thousnads of unemployed men to work during the Depression at that time in the Civilian Conservation Corps (CCC) they were known as "Roosevelt's tree army." The "soldiers" certainly earned their nickname here, planting thousands of spruce and pine trees.

Today the land makes up part of six state forests. The *Six Nations Trail System*, a series of loops and spurs designed for equestrians and snowmobiles, covers nearly 45 miles.

Schuyler County

Phone Number
- None

Website
- nysparks.state.ny.us/parks/info.asp?parkID=104

Admission Fee
- None

Park Hours
- Daylight hours

**Nearest Finger Lake
- east of Keuka**

Directions
- *Sugar Hill Recreation Area*; on Sugar Hill Road off Route 226, between Bradford and Tyrone.

The Walks

If you are going out horseback riding with your dog this is the place to come. Most of the *Six Nations Trail System* courses through the Sugar Hill Forest and the Sugar Hill Recreation Area is a good choice to use as your base of explorations. You can camp here with 16 covered horse stalls and running water.

If you don't feel like competing with the horse crowd, 15 miles of the *Finger Lakes Trail* runs directly through Sugar Hill - an ideal place to hike with your dog and disappear into the woods. Expect a good bit of elevation change but nothing that will bring your dog to his knees.

Trail Sense: The trails are marked and a map is available.

Bonus

The Sugar Hill Fire Tower was built in 1941 by the CCC, and was used until the mid-1980s when aerial detection became more efficient and economical. The tower is 68 feet tall and sits at an elevation of 2100 feet above sea level. It is actually on Sproul Hill, 2.5 miles northwest of the actual location of Sugar Hill. Open to the public, from the top you can see four of the eleven Finger Lakes. The tower appears on the National Historic Lookout Register.

Dog Friendliness
Dogs are allowed across the Six Nations Trail System.

Traffic
Mostly horses, if any. The *Finger Lakes Trail* usually allows foot traffic only, except in a few places where horse are welcomed on.

Canine Swimming
Water is not a strong feature of the Sugar Hill State Forest, an occasional pond or stream depending on how far you hike with your dog.

Trail Time
Many hours possible.

36
Twin Cedars Environmental Area

The Park

The Department of Environmental Conservation brought stewardship into its own backyard in the 1970s with the purchase of farmland adjacent to its offices here. The DEC planted some white pines, enlarged the pond on the property and stocked it with game fish. In the 1980s the area was developed into an outdoor classroom.

The Walks

Your hike with your dog here begins behind the mini nature center housed in the A-frame building. The first thing your dog will notice as she trots along the edge of the pond is the paw-friendly grass - it is almost like hiking down a golf fairway. And the paw-friendly footing will be a dominant theme of your canine hike across this compact trail system.

Livingston County

Phone Number
- 585-226-2466

Website
- None

Admission Fee
- None

Park Hours
- Always open

**Nearest Finger Lake
- northeast of Conesus**

Directions
- *East Avon*; from I-390 take Exit 10 onto Route 5/20 East. The park is on the south side of the road in less than one mile.

At the first junction take a right to dive into the small trails under thick tree cover; the *Woodchuck Trail* that works through a stand of hemlocks and the *Turtle Trail* that visits the soft grounds around the pond. If you head left you climb a small rise to the back of the property on your way to a 1.2-mile circumnavigation of the entirety of Twin Cedars. This ribbon of trail is heavily forested and almost tunnel-like. Complete this loop by making a left turn at every trail junction. Any right will lead you back into the cool shade of the hemlocks.

Trail Sense: The trails are not blazed and the occasional trail junction sign is not posted where it will help you most but there is no such thing as a wrong turn on these fun trails.

Bonus

Everyone is familiar with the dramatic shaping of the Central New York landscape by the mile thick glaciers that covered the region 15,000 years ago.
The most obvious souvenir are the Finger Lakes, of course. Less obvious are little hills that were created when the retreating ice sheet deposited piles of rock and soil here and there. These hillocks are known as drumlins and that is what you will be hiking on with your dog at Twin Cedars.

Dog Friendliness

Dogs are allowed to hike the DEC trails at Twin Cedars.

Traffic

Foot traffic only and it is the norm to not see much of it.

Canine Swimming

There is ample access to the pond when wildfowl isn't around.

Trail Time

About one hour.

Your dog will delight in the paw-friendly trails at Twin Cedars.

37
Havana Glen
Park

The Park

McClure's Glen, now known as Havana Glen, was first made accessible to the public in the summer of 1867 by the construction of walks and the erection of bridges and stairways through its rugged and winding way. From the beauty of the Portal Cascade at the beginning to the dramatic appeareance of Eagle Cliff Falls many folks regarded the Glen the superior in beauty to its more celebrated rival, Watkins Glen, up the road.

The small picnic and camping park at the entrance today has been there since the beginning. Reports of picnic parties with 5,000 attendees were common here back in the day.

Schuyler County

Phone Number
- None

Website
- None

Admission Fee
- $1.00

Park Hours
- 8:00 a.m. to 10:00 p.m.

**Nearest Finger Lake
- south of Seneca**

Directions
- *Montour Falls*; take South Catharine Street (Route 14) south of town. Turn left on Havana Glen Road to the park on the right.

The Walks

OK, this is more a walk than a hike but it is hard to imagine any barks of protest coming from your dog. After a quarter-mile trip pressed against the wall of one of the prettiest short gorges in the Finger Lakes you reach the base of Eagle Cliff Falls. The wide curtain of water falls about 50 feet into a round theater with walls twice as high. And best of all for your dog there is safe and easy access to the plunge pool.

One word of caution. Along the way are two flights of open-grate stairs that may give your dog pause.

Trail Sense: From the lot in the back of the park just follow McClure Creek upstream.

Bonus
Not far away on the north side of Montour Falls,
about 100 feet from Route 14 is Aunt Sarah's Falls.
This 90-foot high hydrospectacular passes over the
15-foot wide crest, free falls about 30 feet, strikes
a ledge and fans out to about 35 feet in width.

Dog Friendliness
Dogs are welcome in Havana Glen Park.

Traffic
If you arrive in non-swimming weather your dog may be the only one in the plunge pool.

Canine Swimming
The plunge pool at the bottom of Eagle Cliff Falls is one of the best doggie swimming pools in the Finger Lakes.

Trail Time
Less than one hour.

Playing in the plunge pool of Eagle Cliff Falls will be your dog's best fun in Havana Glen Park.

38
Seneca Lake State Park/ Lakeshore Park

The Park

The north shore of Seneca Lake has rarely looked as attractive as it does today. The shoreline was cleared of its trees and bushes by the City of Geneva in 1922 to create a parkland. That park would ultimately be transferred to New York State in 1957 to be reborn as Seneca Lake State Park.

The original roadbed for Route 5/20 came right down to the waterline. When the road was relocated in 1987 the shoreline was left as a depository of highway rubble. Since then the city has invested millions of dollars to create Lakeshore Park.

The Walks

Seneca Lake State Park is known mostly as a destination for swimmers and picnic goers. There is no trail system but fun canine hiking is afoot here any-

Ontario County

Phone Number
- (315) 789-2331

Website
- nysparks.state.ny.us/parks/info.asp?parkID=97

Admission Fee
- Vehicle entrance fee at the state park but you can hike for free from Lakeshore Park next door

Park Hours
- Sunrise to sunset

**Nearest Finger Lake
- north shore of Seneca**

Directions
- *Geneva*; From New York State Thruway Exit 42 take Route 14 south into town and a left on Lake Street to the parks on Route 5/20.

way. A paved path hugs Seneca Lake for over two miles between the two parks. About the only thing between your dog and near constant views of the lake are a row of historic willow trees that once lined the old roadway. These arboreal sentinels keep your canine hike shady much of the way.

You will pass a small beach where your dog can hop down to the gravelly sand and the pathway is shouldered by large swaths of greenspace which can be used for dog play or as a hiking surface for a free-form return trip.

Trail Sense: There are distance markers every half-mile and the few stray paths you encounter will not delay you long if you wander down the wrong one.

Bonus
Geneva has long been a hub of education in Central New York. Geneva Academy was founded in 1796 and Geneva College, now Hobart College, was established in 1822. In 1834 Geneva Medical College graduated America's first woman doctor, Elizabeth Blackwell, who would practice in Asheville, North Carolina. Since 1836, one in five Geneva citizens has been a student.

Dog Friendliness

Dogs are welcome in both parks but not allowed in swimming areas.

Traffic

This is a busy trail with joggers, cyclists, rollerbladers and other dogwalkers taking advantage of this hike by the lake.

Canine Swimming

Several places where your dog can enjoy Seneca Lake.

Trail Time

More than one hour to hike the lake path to the end and back.

39
Cayuga
Waterfront Trail

The Park

The first development boom on the Cayuga Waterfront occurred in the early 1800s when there were less than 300 people in Ithaca. The first big product handled at the port was gypsum, a key ingredient in plaster. In Union Springs, Philip Yawger opened a mine and started sending shipments to Ithaca on rafts where the rafts were made into wagons and steered south.

Today Tompkins County and the City of Ithaca have teamed to create The Cayuga Waterfront Trail Initiative. Planned for three stages and an eventual total of six miles, the first two miles opened in Cass Park in 2004.

Cass Park has been patched together over the years by a series of land acquisitions. The greenspace is named after Leon Cass, who became city engineer in 1933 and was responsible for much of West Hill development in Ithaca.

Tompkins County

Phone Number
- (607) 273-1090

Website
- www.cayugawaterfronttrail.com

Admission Fee
- None

Park Hours
- Sunrise to sunset

**Nearest Finger Lake
- south shore of Cayuga**

Directions
- *Ithaca*; 701 Taughannock Boulevard (Route 89) at Cayuga Lake.

The Walks

This is as easy and enjoyable an urban canine hike as you are liable to find in the Finger Lakes. The trail is paved throughout but wide and flat, with a pleasing curve to the route.

In 2004 the *Cayuga Waterfront Trail* (CWT) received a national Rail-Trail Design Recognition Award from the Rails-to-Trails Conservancy and the American Society of Landscape Architects. CWT was recognized for its consistent and creative use of design in the interpretive and directional signs, trail furniture, marketing materials, kiosks and destination points.

Bonus
In Spring 2007 the Chamber of Commerce installed
the first dog-friendly fountain on the *Cayuga
Waterfront Trail*. The lowered fountain was bought with
$4,300 raised through a Bob Dylan Tribute Concert.

You will notice a common design theme in the benches, bridges and other trail features as you walk your dog through Cass Park. Other highlights as you move along are the Inlet Overlook and the Hangar Theater at the north end of the Park. The hangar was built in 1932; this land was once part of the Ithaca municipal airport.

Trail Sense: You can find an information kiosk near the ice rink; mileage markers every quarter-mile.

Dog Friendliness
Dogs are allowed to hike these trails and the park has installed dog care stations along the way.
Traffic
Rollerbladers , cyclists, strollers, joggers - if you are seeking a communal dog walk, this is the place.
Canine Swimming
Best to leave the water to the boats here.
Trail Time
About an hour.

40
Sampson State Park

The Park

This land was once the site of the Seneca Indian town of Ken-dai-a. The Senecas fished the lake and tilled the land until the Revolutionary War when marauding Continental Army troops burned many Iroquois towns like this one. After the war, veterans were given land to settle between Seneca and Cayuga lakes.

With the bombing of Pearl Harbor the Federal government established its second largest naval training station here on the shores of Seneca Lake. The facility was named for Rear Admiral William T. Sampson of Palmyra, New York, the Commander of the American blockade during the Spanish-American War of 1898.

When the war ended, veterans again returned to this area as they had after the Revolution. This time it was to be educated in Sampson State College. But with the coming of the Korean War Sampson was again an active military base, this time for the Air Force. Sampson was decomissioned and became a state park in 1960.

Seneca County

Phone Number
- (315) 585-6392

Website
- nysparks.state.ny.us/parks/info.asp?parkID=100

Admission Fee
- Vehicle entrance fee in season

Park Hours
- Sunrise to sunset

**Nearest Finger Lake
- east shore of Seneca**

Directions
- *Romulus*; the park is on Route 96A, south of the intersection with Route 336 and north of the junction with Route 96.

The Walks

The main canine hiking here will be along the *Sampson Lake Trail* that traces the Seneca Lake shoreline south to the hamlet of Willard. The path is paved but there are generous grass shoulders if your dog doesn't want to pound the pavement for the entirety of this nearly four-mile round trip. The trail actually runs above the level of the lake but there are accesses to the shore every now and then.

Bonus
A military museum opened in the park in 1995,
preserving artifacts from Sampson's war days.
Staffed by volunteers - usually on the weekends -
the historical displays are contained in the brig
of the former base.

Although much of the park is slowing reforesting and the trail is line with trees, this route is devoid of shade much of the hike. The terrain is level throughout.

You can also take your dog on a walking tour of the old base. Not many buildings remain but in their place are large grass fields ideal for a game of fetch or chase.

Trail Sense: There is a park map/brochure available. No trail map is needed but there is a guide to tree identification along the *Sampson Lake Trail*.

Dog Friendliness
Dogs are allowed across the park and in the campground.
Traffic
The *Sampson Lake Trail* is multi-use.
Canine Swimming
There is access to Seneca Lake from the trail and around the marina and boat launch.
Trail Time
More than one hour.

Your dog can still see reminders of Sampson's military past at the park museum.

41
Great Hill
Nature Preserve

The Park

To the Senecas South Hill, the 2,000-foot mountain looming over Canandaigua Lake was known as Nundawao, or "Great Hill." According to Seneca tradition their people emerged from this mountain - Seneca literally translates to "People of the Great Hill."

The hillsides of Souh Hill have always been too steep to comfortably farm but logging has stripped the mountain of its trees in years gone by. In 2000 private donations to the Finger Lakes Land Trust protected over 200 acres of land on the mountaintop. The end of logging will preserve not only the woodland but the water quality of the lake from erosion.

The Walks

Your vehicle will do most of your climbing on South Mountain. Your dog's hiking will be on an old logging road, relatively level but the going can be tough if it is overgrown. The trail stem climbs to the summit area and views of Canandaigua Lake 500 feet below. A side detour exists to explore more of the Great Hill and can be used to vary your return trip.

Trail Sense: Wayfinding aids are scarce; a blaze on the side trail helps a bit.

Yates County

Phone Number
- None

Website
- www.fllt.org/protected_lands/protected_lands1.php?id=25

Admission Fee
- None

Park Hours
- Daylight hours

**Nearest Finger Lake
- east of Canandaigua**

Directions
- *Middlesex*; from the town center, take Route 245 South. Continue 4.8 miles and turn right on Sunnyside Road. Go over the West River for .4 miles and bear left at the fork in the road. Go .4 miles to the next fork and bear right onto South Hill Road (unpaved). Go .7 miles up the hill to the entrance to the preserve on the left side of road, marked only be a small green and white sign.

Bonus

Retreating glaciers did more than scrape the Finger
Lakes out and sculpt the steep-sided South Hill.
The melting ice also carried massive boulders great
distances and deposited them willy nilly. Known as
glacial erratics, you can see several here.

Dog Friendliness

Dogs are allowed throughout the preserve.

Traffic

There is only parking space for one car at the trailhead but if that spot is occupied it is possible to park at the bottom of Great Hill in the Hi Tor Wildlife Management Area lot and hike up South Hill Road.

Canine Swimming

There is no swimming on the Great Hill for your dog but on your way out you can stop at the West River fishing access lot for a refreshing dip; if your dog is really feeling frisky you can stop at that Hi Tor lot and hike up Clark's Gully for an encounter with a waterfall.

Trail Time

About one hour.

42
Hemlock and Canadice Lakes Watershed

The Park

Of the eleven Finger Lakes, Hemlock Lake and Canadice Lake, the smallest of the Fingers, are the only two whose shorelines remain undeveloped. That is a direct by-product of an outbreak of cholera and other diseases in 1876 caused by the City of Rochester's poor water quality, then supplied mainly by cisterns. The City guaranteed a supply of fresh water by purchasing 7,100 acres of land around the two lakes. A filtration plant at the north end of Hemlock Lake filters and purifies as many as 48 million gallons of water per day before it is piped to Rochester. The City began reforesting the watershed in 1902, planting three million trees over the next 30 years. By 1947 Rochester had purchased all the existing cottages on the lakeshores and removed them to insure the purity of its water supply.

The Walks

You have several options to explore the undisturbed shorelines around these two lakes. A number of short trails can

Livingston

Phone Number
- None

Website
- www.cityofrochester.gov/watershedpermit.htm

Admission Fee
- None, but a free access permit must be carried with you at all times on the property. The permits are on the front of the brochure that can be picked up in the self-service park kiosk in the parking lot on your left when you enter.

Park Hours
- Daylight hours

**Nearest Finger Lake
- north end of Hemlock**

Directions
- *Hemlock*; From Route 5/20 take Route 15A south out of Lima for 10 miles past the town of Hemlock. After passing the intersection with Route 20A the park will be on the right, at the northern outlet of Hemlock Lake.

be had on the northwest side of Hemlock Lake - these travel through the varied hardwoods on old town roads but don't actually engage the lake. Remember, the City of Rochester is in the business of providing water, not grooming trails so the paths can be unruly when you visit.

Bonus
At the south end of nine-mile long Hemlock Lake you can make an easy canine hike to County Line Falls from a parking lot on Johnson Hill Road.
Take off down an old logging road and in less than one-half mile you will reach the crest of 35-foot Upper County Line Falls, guarded by a phalanx of mature hemlock trees.

Longer one-way, out-and-back dirt trails do trace the shore - down the east shore of Hemlock Lake and the west shore of Canadice. The Canadice Lake route covers the entire three-mile length of the Finger Lake's smallest lake. Hemlock Lake Park at the north outlet is also a fine place for a picnic or game of fetch with your dog.

Trail Sense: A park map is available on the back of the permit brochure, the trailheads are marked and some trails are blazed with tin shields.

Dog Friendliness

Dogs are allowed to use the trails around Hemlock Land and Canadice Lake. Remove any poop within 100 feet of the lakes to keep it that way.

Traffic

No horses or motorized off-road vehicles and little competition for these trails otherwise.

Canine Swimming

No contact with the water for your dog.

Trail Time

Several hours of trail time are available.

43
Bahar Nature Preserve

The Park

John H. Carpenter arrived in this area with his father in 1823 and started New Hope Mills (that still grinds first-rate pancake flour today). Carpenter also opened a distillery at the falls that bear his name. Legend has it that employees would dodge the revenuers who came calling by pushing kegs out the back door and dumping them over the 90-foot falls.

The land first came to the Finger Lakes Land Trust in 1998 when Dawn Bahar sold her 25 acres of family land around a striking 100-foot ravine at a drastically under-market price to preserve it for all time. In 2005 the land trust purchased the property around Carpenter's Falls after it was listed for sale by private owners.

Cayuga County

Phone Number
- None

Website
- www.fllt.org/protected_lands/protected_lands1.php?id=33

Admission Fee
- None

Park Hours
- Sunrise to sunset

**Nearest Finger Lake
- west shore of Skaneateles**

Directions
- *Skaneateles*; Take Route 41A out of town down the west side of Skaneateles Lake. Turn left on Appletree Point Road (there is a green sign for a Millard Fillmore picnic area) and continue 1.6 miles to a parking area on the left.

The Walks

There are a trio of disjointed canine hikes at Bahar - and you may wind up spending most of your time guiding your dog down a steep, twisting, S-shaped road from the parking area to the trailhead. There are blind curves and although there is not much traffic, it only takes one overly aggressive driver...

At the bottom of the road you begin your canine hike back up the Bear Swamp Creek ravine on the remains of the *Old Jug Path*, so named since barrels of spirits were carried from the distillery to the lake along this route. Today the old cart road is often overgrown but passable. Your hike ends at the top of the hill, engulfed by dark hemlocks and gazing into the handiwork carved by the

Bonus

In 1871 Henry Sayles, an employee of the distillery, was tried for the murder of William Dennis, a deputy sheriff who may have been trying to dispense law and order around Carpenter's Falls. After a trial Sayles was acquitted of the crime but it did not matter.
He committed suicide in jail or shortly thereafter.

stream. You will now be surrounded by private property so you will need to take your dog back down the gorge trail and back up that nasty road. The whole adventure will cover less than one mile but is likely to leave you and your dog panting.

To see Carpenter's Falls, drive back to a small turn-off that you passed on the way in, where the road forks. Carpenter's Falls, a 90-foot ribbon of water that squeezes through a notch in 10' thick limestone caprock, is reached with a short quarter-mile trail to the west. Although short, this is a hike only for calm dogs. You will be making your way along a shale-encrusted footpath cut narrowly into a steep, unprotected hillside with a long drop-off.

The lower falls are reached via a difficult hike, about .5 miles from the trail-head. If you have confidence in your dog you can make it to the plunge pool and enjoy a swim right under the falls in a 6' deep pool.

Trail Sense: There is a small information board at Carpenter's Falls; the *Old Jug Path* is blazed and orange flags direct the way to the falls .

Dog Friendliness
Dogs are allowed to hike these trails.
Traffic
Foot traffic only and little of that.
Canine Swimming
Bahar Preserve features a sliver of 65-foot lakeshore that happens to be the only public access to Skaneateles Lake in Cayuga County.
Trail Time
More than one hour.

"Dogs' lives are too short. Their only fault, really."
- Agnes Sligh Turnbull

44
Rush
Oak Openings

The Park

An "oak opening," or "oak savannah," is one of the rarest natural communities in North America. An oak opening occurs naturally where native prairie meets hardwood forest and prairie grasses mingle with the trees.

Development and fire suppression have eradicated more than 99% of the original oak openings in the United States. Fewer than two dozen remain, mostly in the Midwest, and the Rush Oak Openings is the easternmost remaining oak opening and the only one intact in New York. It survived thanks to an underlying base of limestone so close to the surface that it repelled any plow sunk into the soil.

This ecological treasure is preserved by a coalition between the Nature Conservancy, the New York State Department of Environmental Conservation, the Town of Rush and the concerns of private owners.

Monroe County

Phone Number
- None

Website
- None

Admission Fee
- None

Park Hours
- Sunrise to sunset

**Nearest Finger Lake
- south of Conesus**

Directions
- *Rush*; from I-390 Exit 11 take Route 15 South. Parking is available on the left past Honeoye Falls-Five Points Road and by turning left on Honeoye Falls-Five Points Road to a parking area on the right.

The Walks

There are is over 200 acres to explore with your dog in the oak opening on two tracts donated by the Quinn family and the Goff family. The first priority of property managers is to insure the health of the plants, not groom trails for recreation so do not be surprised if your dog has to plow through high grass to follow the trails. Other times, if you arrive after a recent trail mowing, the Oak Openings may resemble a municipal park. Either way, come with a mind to explore.

Bonus
Although the land looks natural it is aggressively managed to maintain the oak opening.
The property requires frequent burning to re-establish and maintain the fire dependent grasses.
The fires also help sun-thirsty oaks and clears the groundcover of leaf litter to make room for the next generation of trees. Look for evidence of recent burns during your visit.

The preferred time to visit is late summer when the trails are drier and the grasses have matured to golden yellow whisps against the aboreal backdrop. Spring brings wildflowers to the grassland areas which alternate with stands of trees on your canine hike. Not much elevation here to challenge your dog, gentle grades tame to 50-foot rise across the oak openings.

Trail Sense: None. Due to periodic burning to maintain the community there are no markers on the property.

Dog Friendliness
Dogs are allowed in the Oak Openings.

Traffic
No bikes or horses here; the small parking lots will guarantee low visitation.

Canine Swimming
None.

Trail Time
About one hour.

45
Keuka Lake State Park

The Park

John Nicholas Rose set out for Yates County in 1823. Once here he purchased over one thousand acres from Captain John Bedoe, paying $8 per acre for his land. In 1829, he married Jane E. Macomb, niece of John Macomb, Jr., one of the architects for the New York City Hall.

Rose made good use of the architectural talent that came in his merger with the Macomb family. He built Esperanza Mansion, the largest house ever built in Yates County. His brother, Henry, and a nephew, Robert Rose, each built a mansion nearby, Henry building "Hampstead," a short distance north, and Robert building "The Chestnuts." At one time the Rose family owned all the land around and between the family mansions.

Yates County

Phone Number
- (315) 536-3666

Website
- nysparks.state.ny.us/parks/info.asp?parkID=37

Admission Fee
- Vehicle entrance fee May to November

Park Hours
- Sunrise to sunset

**Nearest Finger Lake
- north shore of Keuka**

Directions
- *Bluff Point*; the park is at the north end of the west fork of Keuka Lake on Route 54A. Turn south on Pepper Road to the entrance on the right.

In 1967 The Chesnuts was razed to make way for the Keuka Lake State Park. Today the park is a passive recreation destination with facilities for swimming, picnicing and camping.

The Walks

Keuka Lake State Park is not really a hiker's park, more a water-based recreation park. The dominant feature of the park is its campground with 150 sites and the trails mostly serve as foot traffic conduits from the campground to the recreation sites. But that is not to write them off completely. It is easy to combine the narrow pathways into canine hiking loops and give your dog a hearty workout in between swims here. The connecting trails, such as *Yellow* and *Blue*, blast straight uphill and will no doubt set your dog to panting.

Bonus
John Rose completed Esperanza on July 3, 1838.
The Roses had come to the Finger Lakes from the family plantation in Stafford, Virginia and he designed his home to resemble an Antebellum Southern mansion with balanced proportions and classical details firmly rooted in the Greek Revival tradition.
After John Rose died the estate passed through the hands of other distinguished families but the old money ran out in 1922. The county bought the property and used it as the Yates County Poorhouse for a quarter-century before it was closed.
Esperanza suffered dearly at the hands of vandals until it was revived in 1979 as the Chateau Esperanza Winery. You can visit Esperanza today, across the street from the park. It stands as a restaurant/inn.
By the way, the historical photograph of Esperanza that is most often published features a dog on the front lawn. Looks like a springer spaniel.

The quietest and best canine hiking at Keuka Lake State Park is south of the campground around West Bluff Drive. Here the *Orange Trail* rolls around two stacked loops and the *Green Trail* circles the trees from the the camp road.

Trail Sense: The trailheads are marked and a park map/brochure can be picked up on site.

Dog Friendliness
Dogs are welcome in the park and in the campground.
Traffic
Bicycles are not allowed on the hiking trails.
Canine Swimming
There is access to Keuka Lake for canine aquatics, especially at the beach in the off-season.
Trail Time
About one hour.

46
Charlie Major
Nature Trail

The Park

When the route for the Syracuse & Auburn Railroad was laid out it rolled right past the Village of Skaneateles, five miles to the north. Rather than sit back and watch the future pass them by, village officials incorporated the first Skaneateles Railroad Company on May 16, 1836 with a capital of $25,000. Four years later the lne was open for business with a car pulled by a horse over the crude rails. A plank road replaced the railroad in 1850 that operated until the Skaneateles Railroad Company initiated steam engine service in 1867. It was one of the shortest railroad lines in America.

The right-of-way for the "Old Short Line" has been preserved through the efforts of Charlie Major, a town official who began haunting this area in the 1950s. He devised the idea for converting the old railroad tracks into a nature trail and shepherded it into existence.

Onandaga County

Phone Number
- None

Website
- None

Admission Fee
- None

Park Hours
- Sunrise to sunset

**Nearest Finger Lake
- north of Skaneateles**

Directions
- *Skaneateles*; Take Route 20, Genesee Street, into the center of town and turn onto Jordan Street. Make an immediate left on Fennell Street and follow to Old Seneca Turnpike. Go through the intersection and a small parking lot is on the right side.

The Walks

The *Charlie Major Nature Trail* runs for 1.5 miles between Old Seneca Turnpike and Crow Hill Road. Your dog will trotting across dirt and compacted stone under the shade of a leafy canopy. The quick-stepping Skaneateles Creek will be your companion just about every pawfall of the way. The gentle grade of the railroad keeps this a relaxed pace throughout.

Trail Sense: None needed.

Bonus

It did not take long for early settlers to realize the potential for industry here when they arrived and saw the water drop 100-feet as it poured from Skaneateles Lake. Mills of every sort soon stood shoulder to shoulder beside the surging waterflow. Remnants of some of these operations still exist and can be viewed from the *Charlie Major Nature Trail*.

Dog Friendliness

Dogs are welcome on the *Charlie Major Nature Trail*; poop bags are provided at the trailhead.

Traffic

This is a popular place to bring the dog but it is far enough from the village to make it a special effort to get here so you can usually expect to find a stretch of quiet solitude.

Canine Swimming

Access is problematic at times but there are places your dog can find the water slowing and pooling deep enough for dog paddling, aided by a crumbling mill wall here and there.

Trail Time

About one hour to go out and come back.

47
Cayuga Community College Nature Trail

The Park

Cayuga Community College, under the auspices of the State University of New York, opened its doors in the old James Street Elementary School to 69 freshmen in 1953. Before the decade was out, the school had established new quarters on former farmland on Franklin Street.

A trail system was laid out on the 48-acre campus in the 1970s and the accompanying nature center built in 1983. In 2003 the complex was dedicated to Thomas F. Steenburgh, an educator and dean at Cayuga for thirty years.

The Walks

The main track behind the college is a one-mile, crushed stone path. A natural surface hiking trail weaves through that trail as it travels across an airy woodland - thousands of seedlings have been planted in the natural area over the years. This is easy trotting for your dog with minimal changes in elevation on wide paths.

When you finish your loop there are plenty of open spaces on the adjoining athletic fields where you can walk your dog or play a game of fetch.

Trail Sense: A mapboard is at the trailhead but otherwise you are on your own.

Cayuga County

Phone Number
- None

Website
- None

Admission Fee
- None

Park Hours
- Sunrise to sunset

Nearest Finger Lake
- north of Owasco

Directions
- *Auburn*; downtown, north of Genesee Street (Route 20). From the intersection with Route 5, take 5 North and bear right on Franklin Street. Cayuga Community College is on the left; turn down Spartan Hall Lane between the schools and park in Lot E. The trailhead is behind the parking lot.

Bonus

On the other side of town you can take your dog on a
spirited romp down an abandoned railroad line for
1.6 miles hrough woods, wetlands and woodlands.
So many trees have reclaimed the old rail line that
a model train today would have trouble passing
through the tunnels of branches and leaves.
From West Genesee Street, turn south on Dunning Avenue to a small parking lot on the left, just past
Clymer Street to access the *Auburn-Fleming Trail*.

Dog Friendliness

Dogs are welcome to trot these trails.

Traffic

This little urban natural area attracts plenty of trail users from joggers to
dogwalkers.

Canine Swimming

There is splendid access to two small man-made ponds from low, grassy
banks for a doggie swim.

Trail Time

Less than one mile.

48
Birdseye Hollow County Park

The Park

Birdseye Hollow County Park is tucked into 3,400 acres of a state forest. The park was built beside Birdseye Hollow Wildflower Pond in 1966 when Mud Creek was dammed. The 68-acre lake is dominated by a 200-foot fishing pier that is almost as long as the lake is wide.

The Walks

Standing in the parking lot, facing the lake, the canine hiking will commence through an opening in the woods on your right. A blue-blazed spur trail and the white-blazed *Finger Lakes Trail* conspire to create a 1.8-mile hiking loop. Starting out on the blue path things will likely be squishy under paw if there has been any sort of precipitation lately as you push out along the lakeshore.

This will be an easy amble through light, airy woods for your dog. She should have plenty of energy for a game of fetch on the grassy area beside the lake upon your return.

Trail Sense: There is a mapboard to study before you set out and the trails are well-marked.

Steuben County

Phone Number
- None

Website
- None

Admission Fee
- None

Park Hours
- Sunrise to sunset

Nearest Finger Lake - southeast of Keuka

Directions
- *Bath*; take Route 415 East of town. Turn left on Telegraph Road (Route 16) and another left on Birdseye Hollow Road to the park on the left.

Bonus
Here, deep in the woods you will hike across a small cemetery along Telegraph Road. The town of Bradford was founded by Major Robert Bradford in 1836 and these grave markers date from not long after that.

Dog Friendliness

Dogs are allowed in the county park and in the surrounding state forest.

Traffic

Foot traffic only; but don't be surprised if you complete the loop without seeing another trail user.

Canine Swimming

The park areas around the lake edges are swampy but where the trail gets close to the water a dog-paddling dog will find a swim.

Trail Time

Less than one hour.

49
Willard Wildlife
Management Area

The Park

This land is part of the original Military Tract of central New York, two million acres of bounty land set aside to compensate New York soldiers for their participation in the Revolutionary War. The United States Congress already guaranteed each solider at least 100 acres of wilderness land but New York was having a dickens of a time filling its enlistment quotas and had to up the ante to 500 acres.

Willard Wildlife Management Area was once a part of land the Willard State Hospital used in its farm operations. Planting and harvesting was discontinued in 1963 and the land was transferred to New York State Department of Environmental Conservation for hunting, fishing and recreational use.

Seneca County

Phone Number
- None

Website
- None

Admission Fee
- None

Park Hours
- Sunrise to sunset

**Nearest Finger Lake
- east shore of Seneca**

Directions
- *Ovid*; west of town on Route 96A. Go south on Route 132 and Willard WMA is on the right. Follow the gravel entrance road to the trailhead.

The Walks

Although the park consists of 135 acres of cropland and only 23 acres of woodland, your canine hike here is all in the light forest - a classic woods walk, in fact. The trail is short, the passageway wide and the surface paw-friendly dirt. Your destination is unique in access around the Finger Lakes - a clifftop view of Seneca Lake, the largest of the Finger Lakes and the second deepest body of water wholly contained within the United States.

This is easy going for your dog as the trail slopes gently to Seneca Lake, although a branch trail to the fishing access demands more exertion. You can also take your dog around Willard Wildlife Management's Area's cultivated

Bonus

For half a century, from World War II to the Gulf War, Willard WMA's neighbor was the Seneca Army Depot. Captured within its 24 miles of security fence were several whitetail deer of the normal brown coloration. As the herd grew, it became infiltrated with a few rare individuals of white deer, carrying the recessive gene for white coloration. These are not albinos - they retain a typical deer's brown eyes. The U.S. Army protected the white deer protection while they managed the brown deer through hunting. Today the military has gone but the white deer remain behind the fence - the world's largest and only herd of white deer, nearly 200 individuals strong. Seneca White Deer, Inc. oversees the property and they will likely begin offering regular wildlife bus tours to see the white deer in 2008. Don't expect your dog to be invited, however.

fields. One of the unique things your dog will encounter will be a pair of pothole ponds.

Trail Sense: None; no maps on site or signs for the trailhead or markings for the trail. But there should be no need to summon the St. Bernards to rescue anyone on the thin slice of parkland.

Dog Friendliness
Dogs are allowed throughout the wildlife management area.
Traffic
Little.
Canine Swimming
Those pothole ponds are awfully inviting, with unvegetated banks all around.
Trail Time
Less than one hour.

50
High Vista
Preserve

The Park

This hillside forest was once typically barren of trees right down to the edge of Skaneateles Lake. The trees came back, humans moved on and the Nature Conservancy became steward of the land. They gave the 120-acre property to the non-profit High Vista, Inc. organization but when the oufit closed shop the land came back to the Nature Conservancy. In 1993 they donated it one more time, handing it over to the Finger Lakes Land Trust.

The Walks

You begin your canine hike at High Vista by walking downhill on the dirt road. You'll catch glimpses of Skaneateles Lake through the trees to your right, and if it is lake views you seek you should be here when the leaves are down. Look closely for the unmarked trailhead on your left just after you cross the creek. There is a small green sign and the trademark New York state boulders at the trailhead.

Onandaga County
Phone Number - None
Website - www.fllt.org/protected_ lands/protected_lands1. php?id=23
Admission Fee - None
Park Hours - Sunrise to sunset
Nearest Finger Lake - southeast of Skaneateles
Directions - *Scott*; From Route 41, turn onto Vincent Hill Road West, just north of the Cortland/ Onondaga County line. The small parking area is on the right, just before the paved portion of the road expires.

The route is a lollipop trail that ascends moderately along a tumbling stream and then loops around the water. Hemlocks predominate in the gully around the stream but the narrow dirt band of trail can be overwhelmed by a vibrant understory that grows under the mixed hardwoods.

Trail Sense: A park map can be downloaded from the website but nothing is available on-site. The string trail to the loop is blazed in yellow; the loop in blue - but look closely for the paint swaths.

Bonus
The preserve has been designated as an Important Bird Area by the Audubonn Society for its abundance of songbirds nesting in the deciduous forest canopy. One resident of interest is the cerulean warbler, the species of warbler presently in sharpest decline due to habitat destruction. It migrates farther and earlier, and forages and nests higher in the canopy than many other warbler species. The adult male is a deep cerulean blue above with a streaked back, and is white below with a narrow blue-black band across the throat.

Dog Friendliness
Dogs are welcome to hike this woodsy loop.

Traffic
Little if any.

Canine Swimming
Only splashing in the streams.

Trail Time
About one hour.

The sounds of this energetic stream are with your dog throughout most of your hike in the High Vista Preserve.

Camping With Your Dog In The Finger Lakes

Babcock Hollow Campground
Bath
At 5932 Babcock Hollow Road, south of Route 415 east of town .
open nid-May to mid-October (607) 776-7185

Back Archers Campsites
Himrod
At 3112 Route 14.
open May to October (607) 243-7926

Bristol Woodlands Campground
Bristol
From Canandaigua go west on Route 5/20 and turn south on Route 64. Turn right onto CR 32 in Bristol Center for 1.5 miles to South Hill Road. **open May 1 to October 20** (585) 229-2290

Buttermilk Falls State Park
Ithaca
On route 13 south of town.
open May 1 to November 30 (607) 272-1886

Camp Bell Campground
Campbell
At 8700 Route 415, 1.2 miles north of Route 17
open May 1 to October 31 (607) 527-3301

Campers Haven
Bath
In town on Route 15 at 6832 Knight Settlement Road.
open May 1 to mid-October (607) 776-0328

Canandaigua/Rochester KOA

Farmington
From Route 5/20 take 332 north 5 miles, right on Farmington Townline Road.
open April 1 to October 31   (585) 398-3582

Cardinal Campground

Campbell
From Route 17 Exit 41 turn on County Route 333 over the tracks to Campbell. Turn left at gas station and go 3.7 miles to Thurston. Turn right CR 12 and right on Dee Road.
May 5 to October 1   (607)527-8152

Cayuga Lake State Park

Seneca Falls
On Route 89, 3 miles south of Route 5/20.
open May 1 to November 1   (315) 568-1261

Cheerful Valley Campground

Phelps
On Route 14, .75 miles north of I-90 Exit 42.
open April 15 to October 15   (315)781-1222

Clute Memorial Park and Campground

Watkins Glen
On Seneca Lake at 155 S. Clute Park Drive (Route 414).
open May 1 to November 1   (315) 497-0130

Conesus Lake Campground

Conesus
At 5609 East Lake Road, 5.75 miles south of Route 20A, 2.5 miles east of I-390 Exit 8.
open May 15 to October 15   (585) 346-2267

Cool-Lea Campground

Odessa
On Route 228, 3 miles from Route 224 off Route 13.
open May 15 to October 15   (607) 594-3500

Cross Lake Park Campground
Cato
12946 Dugar Road, .7 mile south of SR 370 from the junction of SR 370 and SR 34
open May 1 to October 1   **(315) 678-2143**

Fillmore Glen State Park
Moravia
5283 Deep Hole Road, north of town off Maddox Boulevard.
open May 1 to November 1   **(315) 497-0130**

Finger Lakes National Forest – Blueberry Patch Campground
Hector
On CR2, east of Route 414, .5 miles north of ranger station.
open May 1 to October 31   **(607) 546-6670**

Four Winds Campground
Portageville
7350 Tenefly Road, one miel south of Griffith Road, 1.7 miles from the Letchworth State Park entrance.
open early May to early October   **(585) 493-2794**

Havana Glen Park
Montour Falls
south of town on Havana Glen Road off Route 14.
open May 1 to November 1   **(607) 535-9476**

Hejamada Campground
Montezuma
From Route 5/20 turn left onto Route 90. At stop sign turn right and then left onto McDonald Road.
open May 1 to October 15   **(315) 776-5887**

Hickory Hill Camping Resort
Bath
At 7531 Haverling Street (CR 13), two miles north of Route 54 and one mile north of Route 17, Exit 38
open May 1 to October 31   **(607) 776-4345**

Holiday Hill Campground
Springwater
From Route 15 south of town go east on Walker Street and left on Strutt Street.
open early May to early October **(585) 669-2600**

Junius Ponds Cabins & Campground
Phelps
On West Townline Road off Route 318, .75 miles from I-90, Exit 42.
open open April 15 to October 15 **(315)781-5120**

Keuka Lake State Park
Keuka Park
At 3370 Pepper Road off Route 54A, 6 miles west of town.
open May 1 to November 30 **(315) 536-7356**

Lansing Park
Lansing
On Myers Road off Route 34B.
open mid-May to mid-October **(607) 533-7388**

Letchworth State Park
Perry
6 miles south of Mount Morris entrance (Route 36).
open May 1 to November 1 **(585) 237-3303**

Ontario County Park at Gannett Hill
Bristol Springs
West Gannett Hill Road from Route 64 north of town.
open Memorial Day to Labor Fay **(585) 374-6250**

Otisco Lake Campground
Marietta
At 1544 Otisco Valley Road (Route 174) south of town.
open mid-May to mid-October **(315) 636-9925**

Paradise Park Campground
Reading Center
At 4150 Cross Road off Church Road west of Rout 14A.
open May 1 - mid-October **(607) 535-6600**

Pinecreek Campground
Newfield
28 Rockwell Road off Hines Road from Route 327, four miles from Route 13.
open May 1 to October 15   (607) 273 1974

Robert H. Treman State Park
Ithaca
Route 327 east of Route 13.
open May 1 to November 1   (607) 272-1886

Sampson State Park
Romulus
At 6096 Route 96A north of Willard.
open May 1 to November 1   (315) 585-6392

Skybrook Campground
Dansville
norht of town on Route 36, .3 mile west on Route 436, south on Ossian Road and follow signs to 10861 McCurdy Road.
open May 1 to October 1   (585) 335-6880

Sned-Acres Family Campground
Ovid
On Route 89, north of Route 138.
open April 15 to November 1   (607) 869-9787

Southern Shores Campground
Conesus
At 5707 East Lake Rd south of Route 5/20, east from I-390 Exit 8.
open May 1 to November 1   (585) 346-5482

Spruce Row Campsite
Ithaca
Take Route 96A north from Ithaca 7 miles to Jacksonville Road; turn right for 1 mile to Kraft Road and turn right for 1.5 miles.
open May 1 to Columbus Day   (607) 387-9225

Stony Brook State Park
Dansville
On Route 36, south of I-390 Exit 4.
open year-round **(585) 335-8072**

Sugar Creek Glen Campground
Dansville
From I-390 Exit 4 take immediate right at sign and go five miles to 11288 Poags Hill Road.
open April 28 to October 15 **(585) 335-6294**

SunSet-on-Seneca Campsites
Lodi
At 8449 Lower Lake Road, from Lodi Point Road off Route 136 west of town.
open April 15 to October 15 **(607) 582-6030**

Taughannock Falls State Park
Ithaca
On Route 89, north of town.
open year-round **(607) 387-6739**

Tumble Hill Campground
Cohocton
On SR 371, .5 miles north of Route 415 from I-390 Exit 2.
open May 1 to October 31 **(585) 384-5248**

Watkins Glen-Corning KOA Kampground
Watkins Glen
At 1710 Route 414, 4.5 miles south of Route 14.
open mid-April to November 1 **(607) 535-7404**

Watkins Glen State Park
Watkins Glen
Off Franklin Street (Route 14) in town at 3530 Route 419.
open May 1 to November 1 **(607) 535-7666**

Vickio's Deerfield Park

Watkins Glen

3378 CorningStreet (Route 329) off Route 14 in town.

open May 1 to October 15   **(585) 335-8072**

Wigwam Keuka Lake Campground

Bluff Point

At 3324 Esperanza Road off Route 54A.

open May to November   **(315) 536-6352**

Yawger Brook Family Campground

Auburn

from Route 5/20 go 7 miles west to Blanchard Raod and 1 mile south to Benham Road then .7 miles south to 989 Chamberlain Road.

open May 1 to November 1   **(315) 252-8969**

Index To Parks

Printed in the United States
202211BV00006B/1-51/A